EAST TEXAS HISTORICAL JOURNAL

http://www.easttexashistorical.org

EXECUTIVE DIRECTOR AND EDITOR

M. Scott Sosebee

Carolyn White
Graduate Assistant Editor

VOLUME XLIX   NUMBER 2

FALL 2011

Copyright © 2011 by the East Texas Historical Association. All rights reserved. Reproduction, whether in whole or part, without permission is strictly prohibited.

Vol. XLIX   FAll 2011   Number 2
ISBN: 978-1-936205-52-3

The East Texas Historical Journal is published biannually by Stephen F. Austin State University Press. Address correspondence, unsolicited material, membership queries to The East Texas Historical Association, Scott Sosebee, Executive Director and Editor, P. O. Box 6223, Stephen F. Austin State University, Nacogdoches, TX 75962 Telephone 936-468-2407; e-mail: sosebeem@sfasu.edu; Internet: http://www.easttexashistorical.org.

Manuscripts are read year-round and will not be returned unless accompanied by a self-addressed, stamped envelope.

Cover: Photograph courtesy of Sterling Memorial Library, Yale
         University, New Haven, CT
Printed in the United States of America
Set in Adobe Garamond Pro.

EAST TEXAS HISTORICAL ASSOCIATION
2010-2011 OFFICERS

Tom Crum	President
Cynthia Beeman	First Vice President
Bruce Glasrud	Second Vice President
Christal Gill	Secretary/Treasurer

DIRECTORS

Cynthia Devlin	Zavalla	2011
Mary Kelley Scheer	Beaumont	2011
Portia Gordon	Nacogdoches	2011
George Cooper	Spring	2012
Mary Lenn Dixon	College Station	2012
Charles Grear	New Braunfels	2013
Bernadette Pruitt	Huntsville	2013
Joe Atkins	Dallas	2013
Ted Lawe	Dallas	ex-President
Milton Jordan	Georgetown	ex-President
Archie P. McDonald	Nacogdoches	Life Director
Cissy Lale	Ft. Worth	Life Director

EDITORIAL BOARD

Gene Preuss	Houston
Charles Grear	New Baunfels
Chuck Parsons	Luling
Charles Waite	Edinburg
Steven Short	Dallas
Jere Jackson	Nacogdoches
Gary Pinkerton	Silsbee
Jeff Guinn	Ft. Worth
Paul Sandul	Nacogdoches
John Caraway	Clyde
Gwen Lawe	Dallas

EAST TEXAS HISTORICAL ASSOCIATION
MEMBERSHIP

INSTITUTIONAL MEMBERS pay $100 annually
LIFE MEMBERS pay $400 or more
PATRONS pay $75 annually
BENEFACTORS pay $60 annually

STUDENT MEMBERS pay $15 annually
FAMILY MEMBERS pay $45 annually
REGULAR MEMBERS pay $35 annually

Journals $7.50 per copy
Address: P.O. Box 6223
Stephen F. Austin State University
Nacogdoches, TX 75962
936-468-2407
sosebeem@sfasu.edu

Books Reviewed

Hacker and Mauk, *On the Prairie of Palo Alto: Historical Archaeology of the U.S-Mexican War Battlefield*, reviewed by Pamela Ringle

Carlson and Crum, *Myth, Memory and Massacre: The Pease River Capture of Cynthia Ann Parker*, reviewed by Bill O'Neal

Kelley, *Los Brazos de Dios: A Plantation Society in the Texas Borderlands 1821-1865*, reviewed by Rick Sherrod

Kearney, *Nassau Plantation: The Evolution of a Texas German Slave Plantation*, reviewed by Matthew Tippens

Howell, *Texas Confederate, Reconstruction Governor: James Webb Throckmorton*, reviewed by Sean Cunningham

Stone, *The Chosen Folks: Jews on the Frontiers of Texas*, reviewed by Son Mai

Hoy, *Cowboy's Lament: A Life on the Open Range*, reviewed by Tom Crum

Case, *The Great Southwest Railroad Strike and Free Labor*, reviewed by Kyle Wilkison

Sanders, *Calvin Littlejohn: Portrait of a Community in Black and White*, reviewed by Theodore M. Lawe

Wooten, *The Polio Years In Texas: Battling a Terrifying Unknown*, reviewed by Bobby H. Johnson

Watt, *Farm Workers and the Churches: The Movement in

California and Texas, reviewed by David Urbano

McArthur and Smith, *Texas Through Women's Eyes: The Twentieth-Century Experience,* reviewed by Mary L. Scheer

Lashley Lopez, *Don't Make Me Go To Town: Ranchwomen of the Texas Hill Country,* reviewed by Leslie Daniel

Utley and Beeman, *History Ahead: Stories beyond the Texas Roadside Markers,* reviewed by Paul J. P. Sandul

Graham, *State of Minds: Texas Culture and Its Discontents,* reviewed by Preston Blevins

Medrano, *Americo Paredes: In His Own Words, an Authorized Biography,* reviewed by Ana Luisa Martinez-Catsam

Pick, *Constructing the Image of the Mexican Revolution: Cinema and the Archive,* reviewed by Jason Dormady

Smith, *Until They Are Home, Bringing Back the MIAs from Vietnam, a Personal Memoir,* reviewed by Cynthia Devlin

↩ CONTENTS ↪

REVISITING THE BATTLE OF BAYTOWN: ↪ 9
UNIONS, REDS, AND MAYHEM IN A COMPANY
                   Michael Botson

TWICE THROUGH THE GLASS CEILING: SUE BIRDWELL ALVES   ↪ 24
                 Cynthia Devlin

NARRATIVE OF NEGLECT: TEXAS PRISONS FOR MEN   ↪ 44
          J. Keith Price and Susan Coleman

"WE JUST COME IN TO SEE THE SHOW:"   ↪ 69
VELMA PATTERSON'S SENSATIONAL 1936 HUNT COUNTY MURDER
                  John Hanners

TOGETHER THEY WON: SAM RAYBURN AND THE FOURTH   ↪ 82
CONGRESSIONAL DISTRICT DURING WORLD WAR II
               William McWhorter

INTERPRETING MR. SAM AT HOME: IS IT ENOUGH,   ↪ 94
OR WHY CAN'T IT BE ALL ABOUT MR. SAM?
            Carlyn Copeland Hammons

EAST TEXAS HISTORICAL ASSOCIATION BOOK NOTES   ↪ 102
              Archie P. McDonald

BOOK REVIEWS   ↪ 108

Revisiting the Battle of Baytown: Unions, Reds, and Mayhem in a Company Town

By Michael Botson

In their 1958 monumental history of Baytown's Humble Oil and Refining Company, prominent business historians Henrietta Larson and Kenneth Porter devoted only fifty of their study's 769 pages to the company's labor history. Unsurprisingly, as business historians they focused their attention on the men who established and managed the company rather than the employees who worked there.[1] In summing up the defeat of two union organizing drives between 1936 and 1943, they concluded that "Humble employees simply were not interested in an outside union. They had become convinced that their own federations were effective agencies for collective bargaining with management."[2]

Moreover, Larson and Porter dismissed critics who suggested employees' loyalty to Humble Oil smacked of feudalism and that they were somehow "inferior in stamina to other oil companies' employees who, in the face of more serious attempts at [management] coercion, had organized and won bargaining rights for Oil Workers International locals."[3]

However, their simplistic conclusion leaves unanswered one important question: How, in fact, did Humble Oil and Refining Company defeat two Congress of Industrial Organization (CIO) organizing campaigns during the union's peak popularity while workers in all other major refineries along the upper Texas Gulf Coast successfully organized powerful CIO unions and secured collective bargaining rights?

Several factors affect the answer to this dilemma. First is Humble Oil's tradition of anti-unionism reflected in the labor relations philosophy of its conservative, southern founders, Ross Sterling, Walter

---

Michael Dotson is a Professor of History at Houston Community College, Northwest. He writes and researches on labor issues in Texas. His most recent publication is "Looking for Lefty: Liberal/Left Activism and Texas Labor, 1920-1960s" with George Norris Green in The Texas Left: The Radical Roots of Lone Star Liberalism," David O'Donald Cullen and Kyle G. Wilkison, editors.

Fondren, Robert Blaffer and William Farish. Under their leadership the company crushed its employees' first union organizing campaign during the Goose Creek Oil Field Strike in 1917.[4] In 1920 Humble Oil and Refining became part of John D. Rockefeller's Standard Oil Corporation of New Jersey and adopted Standard's antiunion policy as laid out under the Colorado Industrial Relations Plan.[5] The plan consisted of four elements: a corporate welfare system, a grievance procedure, an employees' bill of rights, and lastly Joint Councils, eventually called Employee Representation Plans, which contained employee elected representatives along with management appointed members.

C.S. Stone, the first person hired to work for Humble oil in Baytown leading a yoke of oxen hauling heavy equipment to the refinery construction site, circa 1917. Photo courstesy of Sterling Memorial Library, Yale University New Haven, CT.

The Plan appeared to establish joint governance between management and employees, but the agreements formulated in the Council lacked substance because they were not the result of negotiations between two parties which held equal power and had learned to respect each other's economic strength. As a result there was never any agency to compel employers to honor agreements reached through the Joint Council.[6] Paternalistic in nature and anti-union in objective, the Plan allowed management to retain control over industrial relations with an iron fist as demonstrated when Humble Oil's Joint Conference figured prominently in management's defeat of the CIO's organizing drive in 1936. In addition to the Joint Conference, other factors led to the CIO's defeat, including managements, intimidation of CIO members, and alliance of anti-union local businessmen, their trade associations and newspaper editors who rallied against the CIO, "Red" and race baiting, and, finally, the Union's misguided decision to call a strike.

The battle between pro- and anti-union factions in Baytown actually dated back to 1934 when Humble employees Bob Oliver and Roy Childers first established Local No. 333 of the Oil Workers Union affiliated with the American Federation of Labor (AFL). At the time the union claimed 1,400 members, approximately sixty percent of Humble's 2,300 employees. Oliver requested a union certification election under the authority of the Section 7(a) of the National Industrial Recovery Act (NIRA). Management refused to hold an election based on its opposition to recognizing the union as the sole collective bargaining agent for its employees. Local No. 333 responded by appealing to the Petroleum Labor Policy Board to certify the union without an election but before the Board could take any action the Supreme Court declared the NIRA unconstitutional in May, 1935 thus making the issue mute.[8]

Local No. 333 abandoned the AFL in 1936 over philosophical and organizing differences, and they affiliated with the newly formed CIO. Although employees expressed continuing interest in the union, they remained well-aware that the company disdained it. Twice between September, 1935, and March, 1936, management refused to meet with Oliver and Childers to discuss union recognition, wages, promotions, and seniority rights. The company took the position that in these matters management would only consider individual cases and would not enter into any binding agreement with the Union over these issues or recognize it as the collective bargaining agent for its employees.

Nonetheless, by late summer 1936, the union's growing numbers and potential influence could not be ignored. Consequently, management consented to meet with Oliver, Childers, and other union officials to discuss union recognition, wages, promotions, and seniority rights. Company officials partly met with union representatives because the union's growing presence could not be dismissed, but they also could not ignore the newly passed Wagner Act, which had empowered workers to organize unions. Like other companies at the time, Humble Oil officials were willing to meet with union representatives as a show of complying with the law, while, at the same time, stalling negotiations, hoping the U.S. Supreme Court would rule the Wagner Act unconstitutional in a case filed against it by the Jones & Laughlin Steel Corporation. The meeting took place in the refinery's administrative offices on September 4.[10]

The day before the meeting, management distributed an open letter from executive vice president Harry Weiss that poisoned the atmosphere. In it, he praised the company's harmonious history of labor relations and condemned the CIO organizers as outside agitators determined to cause trouble. Weiss ignored the fact that Humble's employees worked as organizers and that hundreds of employees had joined the CIO. In part the letter proclaimed:

> The leaders of this movement are outsiders who seek to impose their rule on the rest of us. The success of efforts of this kind is dependent upon coercion, and that is the root of the evil. This insidious force can be best combated by the resistance of the employees themselves. The Company will stand behind you with all possible support.[11]

Weiss's letter became the opening broadside against the CIO, even before management met with union officials. It left no doubt in the minds of employees as to the company's attitude towards the union. From that point on, the anti-CIO assault became a highly orchestrated, systematic campaign that ultimately defeated the union's organizing drive in 1936.

The meeting's transcript is an object lesson in obfuscation. Management representatives tied every issue introduced by Bob Oliver and other union officials into linguistic knots, however, one thing does clearly stand out in spite of management's circumlocution, and that was the company's unequivocal refusal to recognize the CIO as the collective bargaining agent of its employees. During the meeting union officials Bob Oliver and C.C. Fogerty pointedly asked the head of management's delegation, D.B. Harris, to sign a contract and recognize the union. Harris refused, saying that, "We are not willing to write a contract . . . We are not willing to sign an agreement to treat your group any differently in any other respect, either better or any worse than the rest of the employees."[12] Harris went further, saying that the company would not recognize any third party as the employees' exclusive collective bargaining agent, and restated its policy to meet with employees on an individual basis to settle any labor disagreements. A policy he noted, which had worked satisfactorily for years.[13] Oliver bitterly disagreed.

He chastised Harris for "[s]etting up [himself] as the man to pass judgment on what is satisfactory or what is not satisfactory. I say to you there is a large percentage of your employees who do not accept it as satisfactory. You know this is a serious situation."[14] Harris responded by hewing to the line that even if Local No. 333 represented one hundred percent of Humble's employees, management would not recognize it or any other organization as their collective bargaining agent. But, in fact, during the previous fourteen years management had "fostered, encouraged and supported the Joint Conference in its refinery and conditioned its employees to collective dealing through it."[15] The meeting ended with this impasse. Outraged at Humble's intransigence and duplicity, Oliver and his organizers responded to management's hardball tactics by re-energizing their organizing efforts.

Almost immediately after the organizing efforts began, a rumor quickly spread throughout Baytown that the CIO would strike if management did not recognize the union. The source of the rumor has never been discovered, but it crippled the CIO's organizing effort by focusing public attention on the potential of a violent strike.[16] It clouded the union's message of trying to cast itself as a responsible and effective employee advocate, making it nearly impossible to cast the CIO in a positive light. The rumored strike forced organizers into curtailing recruiting efforts and into defending the CIO against charges that it was comprised of agitators bent on anarchy in Baytown.

The fear of a potentially violent strike hamstrung the CIO's recruiting efforts and perhaps, even more importantly, convinced many members to drop out of the union. In early August the union claimed 1,400 members; but after the strike rumor spread, membership quickly dropped to approximately 800.[17] Beginning in August and until the union capitulated in September, the strike issue colored the rhetoric hurled back-and-forth by the antagonists, heightening passions in Baytown to the boiling point.

Management ordered foremen to gauge union strength by trying to identify CIO members; to stigmatize them as troublemakers; to voice management's displeasure with union members; and, finally, to intimidate employees undecided about joining the union. Management ordered a garage foreman to conduct a straw poll among his employees to gauge strike sympathy. Foremen throughout the refinery conducted similar polls and directly challenged known CIO organizers and members. In the inspection department, its foreman confronted a union organizer about his union activities, in particular about his recruiting visits to African American employees' homes, an action overstepping the racial boundaries of Jim Crow segregation. The foreman cautioned him, saying, "Well it looks like to me that they are letting you do the dirty work over there . . guiding these Negroes around Baytown . . .That will get you into trouble sooner or later . . .you are letting [union organizers] Bob Oliver and Roy Childers make a sap out of you."[18] The accuracy of these polls is suspect since many CIO members would not publicly acknowledge membership fearing management reprisals. The subtle though unequivocal message management communicated through these polls was that Humble Oil and Refining regarded CIO membership as disloyalty to the company and that those who joined fell from favor and jeopardized their jobs.

An additional factor that hurt the CIO included the Texas Communist Party's support of the union's organizing efforts in Baytown. Texas Communist Party head Homer Brooks praised the CIO as the only "industrial form of organization capable of meeting and defeating the huge financial interests in the mass producing industries such as oil."[19] Brooks' enthusiastic support of the CIO's industrial unionism, his endorsement of the CIO's commitment to racial equality, and his assertion that "[t]he interests of the Party are identical with the labor movement," all played into hands of union critics. Though the Sabine-Houston Branch of the Texas Communist Party voiced support for the CIO's efforts in Baytown, there is no evidence that Homer Brooks or any Communists worked in Baytown as organizers.[20]

The union's call for interracial unionism and the abolition of Jim Crow segregation prompted searing attacks and condemnation of the CIO from racists. Bulletins issued by the Joint Conference's successor organization, the Employees Federation, accurately reflect the hysteria, racist passions, and fear unleashed by race-baiting in southeast Texas during that era. One bulletin warned, "The CIO in its frantic struggle for more votes is secretly carrying on a campaign among Negro workers intended to cause serious trouble . . .They promise that all forms of racial separation shall be abolished . . . We call upon you free white America workers of Baytown refinery to give your active help [to stop this]." Additionally, the arrival in Baytown of African American dockworkers from Houston and other outlying Gulf Coast ports to rally black support for the CIO fanned racial fears among uneasy whites that militant black longshoremen would attack strikebreakers.[21]

Baytown quickly polarized between those supporting the union and those opposed. Raising the banner of preserving law and order, the newly formed Tri-Cities Citizens Committee, composed of anti-union employees, prominent local businessmen, bankers, the Chamber of Commerce, and newspaper publishers, mobilized to marshal public opinion against the CIO. The fiercely anti-union Clifford Bond, influential publisher of the *News Tribune*, used his newspaper as a platform to condemn the CIO.[22] In a bold two-column front page story on September 16, 1936, Bond vilified union president Bob Oliver:

> I have found that a young and ambitious man by the name of Bob Oliver, some three years ago, chose the Tri-Cities area as a fertile field to become a sort of "Czar, Mussolini, Hitler, or what have you?" among the laboring men of the Tri-Cities . . He was able to rally gullible individuals in the employ of the Humble Refinery . . . I have found that after drawing a fat salary from the dues of the members, Mr. Oliver finally reached a point where it became necessary for him to either "deliver the goods or get off the receptacle" (if you get what I mean).[23]

Bond had no qualms about mixing "isms" in his denunciation of Oliver and the union. He fell back on the common anti-union tactic of stereotyping big labor bosses as racketeers who are out to enrich themselves by soaking union members for dues. Other Committee members volunteered to give anti-union speeches, engaged in an aggressive pamphleteering campaign in conjunction with Humble's Security League, and organized mass rallies to coordinate public opinion against the CIO.[24]

The Tri-City Citizens' Committee helped anti-CIO employees organize a back-to-work association in preparation for the strike. The association petitioned local law enforcement agencies to deputize non-striking employees and private citizens so they could protect strikebreakers who crossed CIO picket lines, actions that turned the Baytown refinery into an armed camp. Management began stockpiling food and arranging sleeping accommodations for employees who wanted to remain in the refinery during the strike, and even looked into the feasibility of landing cargo planes on refinery property to keep

Photos on pages 16 and 17 are construction of the refinery's mechanical shops, circa 1919. The tent city in the background housed African American and Mexican laborers. Photos courtesy of Sterling Memorial Library, Yale University, New Haven, CT.

the workforce supplied. By the third week of September, the tension in Baytown had reached a fever pitch, leading to fears of violence.[25] Union activism raised race and class anxieties, the fear of communism led to fears of radicalism, and perhaps most important, the power of Humble Oil and Refining Company hung in the Baytown air like vapors from its refinery, ready to ignite into a full-blown war.

After a promising start, the CIO soon found itself on the defensive and quickly lost ground. To publicize the CIO's position and regain control over the issues, Bob Oliver published a letter in the Houston *Chronicle* laying out the union's objectives in Baytown. The letter reiterated the CIO's demand for recognition as the employees' collective bargaining agent and requested wage increases and seniority to become a basis for consideration in promotions, demotions, transfers ,and layoffs.[26] Management flatly turned down all of Oliver's demands, thereby forcing the union's hand. Oliver then reluctantly called for a strike vote, which the rank-and-file approved with a tally of 787 to 57.[27] The union set September 18 as the strike date. On September 16, the Tri-Cities Citizens' Committee and the Joint Conference placed a half-page ad in the Houston *Chronicle,* proclaiming, "We do not believe there is justification for a strike in the Baytown Refinery."[28] Another article in the same edition cited an unsubstantiated report that 3,100 of the refinery's employees signed an anti-strike pledge circulated by officers of the Joint Conference.[29]

Adding to the CIO's woes was an attack within organized labor. The members of the International Association of Machinists, Local No. 1051 (AFL), which represented skilled machinists in the refinery, opposed the strike. Although the machinists' union only represented Humble's 108 skilled machinists, a small fraction of the overall workforce, its opposition to the strike was a humiliating blow to the CIO by publicly displaying the bitterness within Baytown's house of labor.[30] The machinists' position might have been expected, given that the CIO and AFL were mortal enemies stemming from bitter disagreements over racial policies, as well as craft versus industrial union tensions.

The AFL routinely opposed CIO organizing efforts and engaged in race- and Red-baiting against the CIO similar to that of companies and anti-union workers.[31]

Under great pressure, Bob Oliver and members of Local No. 333 rethought the strike amidst rapidly growing disillusionment with the CIO and decided to hold another vote on the eve of the walkout. Its adversaries had whipped up hysteria in Baytown by successfully stigmatizing the union as bent on class warfare, racial radicalism, and communism. In the second vote, the union unanimously decided to call off the strike, thereby ending the first battle for Baytown between pro and anti-union factions and representing a resounding defeat for the CIO.[32] However, was it defeated, as Larson and Porter concluded, due to Humble's employees simply not being interested in a union like the CIO? Upon careful re-examination, the picture appears much more complex.

Pro-CIO employees faced an uphill battle on numerous fronts in their effort to organize the refinery. A plethora of factors, including management's historic anti-unionism dating back to the Goose Creek oil field strike in 1917, its implementation of Standard Oil of New Jersey's labor policies that included the Joint Conference as a means to foster employee loyalty and discourage unionization, cooperation between management and the hastily formed Tri-City Citizens' Committee coordinating community opposition to the CIO, Red- and race-baiting to smear the union, and the strike rumor, all coalesced to defeat the CIO.

It is essential to note that over the key issue that led to the unraveling of the CIO's organizing campaign, the origin of the strike rumor, there is disagreement between Larson and Porter and the official Labor Board records. Larson and Porter suggest the rumor originated from the CIO as a threat to bully the company into recognizing the union without actually going on strike; but in a Labor Board hearing held afterwards, the official record shows that the source of the rumor was never discovered. The nature of this disagreement is critically important in trying to understand the historical significance of the CIO's defeat, since prior to the rumored strike the union enjoyed significant popularity in Baytown, which Larson and Porter recognized.[33]

Furthermore, an announcement of the union's intention to strike ran counter to the CIO's overall national strategy in 1936 and early 1937. Facing reactionary anti-union forces throughout industrial America, similar to the ones encountered in Baytown, CIO leaders understood that a strike should be a last resort for several reasons. Despite the perception of rising worker militancy, solidarity, and class consciousness during the depression, these were not characterizations universally accepted by American workers. Many remained loyal to their companies and company unions, while still others sat-on-the-fence, waiting see whether management or labor prevailed before joining the CIO.[34]

The great Flint sit-down strike against General Motors, from December 1936 to February 1937, is the best example of this; and although it resulted in an unprecedented victory for workers and organized labor, the CIO authorized the strike as a desperate last resort and planned it in complete secrecy. Only a handful of Flint's autoworkers participated in the strike, while large numbers of GM workers opposed, or simply watched with detachment.[35] It was risky business to join a union, and a failed strike would likely cost a striker his job. All of these factors came into play during the CIO's Baytown organizing campaign and drove union president, Bob Oliver, to exclaim in frustration, "Hell, I am opposed to it too. We decided to call the strike as a last resort. What we want is to get the Humble Oil and Refining Company to reason with us."[36]

The strike rumor could very well have emanated from any of Baytown's anti-CIO factions, such as a member of the Tri-Cities Citizens' Committee, the Joint Council, management, or even from an agent provocateur who infiltrated the CIO. The report of the La Follette Civil Liberties Committee, chaired by Wisconsin Senator Robert La Follette, conclusively demonstrated that labor spies from private detective agencies hired by corporations had infiltrated the CIO from its founding, so it is conceivable that the strike rumor could have originated from an agent provocateur or by any of the groups in Baytown opposing the union.[37] This, of course, is an important avenue of future research.

In summing up labor's defeat in the first Battle for Baytown, it is much more complicated than the conclusion of Larson and Porter that employees in Humble's refinery "were not interested in an outside union."[38] An examination and analysis of the forces arrayed against Humble's employees loyal to the CIO and their effort to organize the refinery, it is clear they faced a collection of adversaries who coalesced into an unassailable anti-union front. It is not so much a surprise that they suffered a defeat as it is a wonder how they managed to do as well as they did.

(Endnotes)

[1] Henrietta Larson and Kenneth Wiggins Porter, *History of Humble Oil and Refining Company* (New York: Harper and Brother Publishing, 1959), 66-77, 350-389.

[2] Henrietta Larson and Kenneth Wiggins Porter, *History of Humble Oil and Refining Company.*, 375.

[3] Henrietta Larson and Kenneth Wiggins Porter, *History of Humble Oil and Refining Company.*, 387, 375.

[4] James C. Maroney, "The Texas-Louisiana Oil Field Strike of 1917," In *Essays in Southern Labor History: Selected Papers, Southern Labor History Conference, 1976*, Gary M. Fink and Merl E. Reed, eds., (Westport, CT: Greenwood Press, 1977), 161-172; William Lee Greer, "The Texas Gulf Coast Oil Strike of 1917," Master's thesis, University of Houston, 1974; Larson and Porter, *Humble Oil*, 66-71.

[5] The foremost example of Standard Oil's violent antiunionism occurred in April 1914 when the Colorado Fuel and Iron Company, a subsidiary of Standard was involved in a strike with the United Mineworkers of America that resulted in the Ludlow Massacre, one of the worst tragedies in American labor history when thirty-three people, including two women and eleven children, died at the hands of the Colorado State Militia. Public outrage over the Ludlow Massacre, aimed in large measure at the Rockefellers, sparked a passionate national debate over the violence inherent in American labor relations. The U.S. Industrial Commission on Industrial Relations issued a scathing report in 1915 on the Ludlow killings and suggested a number of prolabor remedies to eliminate such violence, such as the workers right to organize unions. Unsurprisingly, Standard for the most part ignored the report. Nonetheless, determined to overcome the negative publicity that sullied the Rockefeller name, John D. Rockefeller Jr. hired Mackenzie King, a Canadian labor relations expert, to resurrect the family's tarnished image by formulating a labor relations policy for Colorado Fuel and Iron and Standard Oil to eliminate the conditions that led to the Ludlow Massacre. King named the plan the Colorado Industrial Representation Plan.

The Joint Councils were set up to deal with things such as health and sanitation, safety and accidents, recreations, education and conciliation. It is important to note that the Councils only had authority to advise and not make decisions. In practice foremen continued to wield great power over day-to-day labor relations and were in a position to take retribution against employees filing grievances. Consequently, employees avoided filing grievances with Joint Conference representatives out of fear of reprisals from their foreman.

The Colorado Plan did not empower employees though it appeared to establish joint governance between management and employees with the Joint Council. The plan flatly stated, "The right to hire and discharge, the management of properties, and the direction of work forces shall be vested exclusively in the Company, and, this right shall not be abridged." Paternalistic in nature and antiunion in objective, management continued to control industrial relations with an iron fist. The agreements formulated in the Joint Council lacked substance because they were not the result of negotiations between two parties which held equal power and had learned to respect each other's economic strength. As a result there was never any force to compel employers to honor agreements reached through the Joint Council. In 1915 Standard Oil of New Jersey introduced its Joint Council at its Bayonne refinery. When Humble Oil opened its Baytown refinery in 1920 management adopted Standard Oil's Colorado Plan which included the Joint

Conference, its company union. See Scott Martelle, *Blood Passion: The Ludlow Massacre and Class War in the American West*, (New Brunswick: Rutgers University Press, 2007), 146-176; Marilynn S. Johnson, *Violence in the West: The Johnson County Range War and the Ludlow Massacre, A Brief History with Documents*, (Boston: Bedford/St. Martins, 2009), 26, 138; William Lyon Mackenzie King, *Industry and Humanity*, (Toronto: University of Toronto Press, 1988), xi-xii; Robert Dunn, *Company Unions: A Study of Employee Representation Plans, Works Councils and Other Substitutes for Labor Unions* (Chicago: Trade Union Educational League, 1927) 5; David Brody, "The Rise and Fall of Welfare Capitalism," in *Change and Continuity in Twentieth-Century America: The 1920s*, eds. John Braeman, Robert Bremner, and David Brody (Columbus: Ohio State University Press, 1968), 159.

[6] William Lyon Mackenzie King, *Industry and Humanity*, (Toronto: University of Toronto Press, 1988), xii.

[7] In 1915 Standard Oil of New Jersey introduced its Joint Council at its Bayonne refinery. See, Harvey O'Connor, *History of Oil Workers International Union (CIO)*, (Denver: A.B. Hirschfield Press, 1950), 1-3; Bruce Kaufman, "The Case for Company Unions," *Labor History* 41 (August 2000): 322; Division of Industrial Relations, *Characteristics of Company Unions, 1935* (Washington D.C.: Government Printing Office, 1938), 9-10 (hereafter referred to as *Company Unions*). In 1915 and 1916 workers at Standard Oil's Bayonne refinery struck over low wages and supervisory abuse. In the ensuing violence nine strikers were killed and 50 wounded in 1915 and seven were killed in the 1916 strike.

[8] National Labor Relations Board, *Decisions and Orders of the National Labor Relations Board*, 16 (Washington D.C.; Government Printing Office, 1940), 118 (Hereafter cited as *Decisions*); Melvyn Dubofsky, *The State and Labor in Modern America*, (Chapel Hill: The University of North Carolina Press, 2001), 128.

[9] National Archives and Record Administration, College Park, MD, Records of the National Labor Relations Board, RG 25, Case File 684, "Official Report of Proceedings Before the National Labor Relations Board in the Mater of Humble Oil and Refining Company and Oil Workers International Union, Local No. 333 and the Oil Workers International Union, Local No. 316," Exhibit No. 25, 2, (Hereafter cited as NARACP, RNLRB, RG 25).

[10] NARACP, RNLRB, RG 25, Exhibit 25, 1-2; Melvyn Dubofsky, *State and Labor*, 142-151; James Green, "Democracy Comes to Little Siberia: Steel Workers Organize in Aliquippa, Pennsylvania, 1933-1937," *Labor's Heritage*, (Summer, 1993): 4-27.

[11] National Labor Relations Board, *Decisions*, 119.

[12] NARACP RNLB, Exhibit 25-26.

[13] NARACP RNLB., 24-29, Henrietta Larson and Kenneth Wiggins Porter, *Humble Oil*, 367.

[14] NARACP RNLB., 26-27.

[15] National Labor Relations Board, *Decisions* 132.

[16] National Labor Relations Board, *Decisions*, 118, see fn. 6.

[17] Henrietta Larson and Kenneth Wiggins Porter, *Humble Oil*, 371.

[18] National Labor Relations Board, *Decisions*, 121.

[19] Homer Brooks, "Build the Farm Labor Party Now," *The Red Trade Unionist*, March 1936; "Statement of the District Committee of District 20 (Texas-Oklahoma) of the Communist Party on the Problems and Tasks Confronting the Oil Field and Refinery Workers."

[20] Homer Brooks, "Why Trade Unionists Belong in the Communist Party," *The Red Trade Unionist*, Dec. 1935.

[21] Henrietta Larson and Kenneth Wiggins Porter, *Humble Oil*, 371.

[24] NARACP, RNLRB, RG 25, Hearing Transcript, 784.

[23] Clifford M. Bond, "Some Truth About This Strike," the *News-Tribune*, September 16, 1936, p. 1.

[24] National Labor Relations Board, *Decisions*, 120.

[25] Henrietta Larson and Kenneth Wiggins Porter, *Humble Oil*, 372; "Strike Parley of Tri-Cities Group is Vain," *Houston Chronicle*, September 15, 1936, p. 1; "Humble Plant Prepares to Meet Strike," *Houston Chronicle*, September 16, 1936, p. 1.

[26] "Humble Company at Loss to Understand Baytown Strike Talk," *Houston Chronicle,* August 27, 1936, p. 1.

[27] "Humble Turns Down Union's Wage Demands," *Houston Chronicle*, August 29, 1936, p. 1.; "Walkout to Be Carried Out Quietly," *Houston Chronicle*, September 11,1936, p. 1.

[28] "To The Public From Humble Employees," *Houston Chronicle*, September 16, 1936, p. 22.

Revisiting the Battle of Baytown

[29] "To The Public From Humble Employees," *Houston Chronicle*, September 16, 1936, p. 22; Larson and Porter put the number at 2,436 who voted to oppose the strike, see Henrietta Larson and Kenneth Wiggins Porter, *Humble Oil*, 372. Different sources contradict each other over the numbers of votes cast opposing the strike vote and range from 3,100 to 2, 436. The same holds true for CIO membership. Larson and Porter put the union's membership at approximately 800 while the September 18, 1936 edition of the *Houston Chronicle* puts the CIO's membership at 1,200. There is also contradiction between the total number of employees working at Humble's Baytown Refinery that ranges from 3,200 to 3,500 depending on what source is referred to.

[30] "Machinists Vote to Take No Part if Strike Called," *Houston Chronicle*, September 16, 1936, p. 22.

[31] Robert H. Zieger, *The CIO, 1935-1955* (Chapel Hill: The University of North Carolina Press, 1995), 18-21; Melvyn Dubofsky and Foster Rhea Dulles, *Labor in America: A History*, 8th ed. (Wheeling: Harlan Davidson, Inc., 2010), 264-275.

[32] Henrietta Larson and Kenneth Wiggins Porter, *Humble Oil*, 372.

[33] National Labor Relations Board, *Decisions*, 118, see fn. 6; Porter and Henrietta Larson and Kenneth Wiggins Porter, *Humble Oil*, 371.

[34] Robert H. Zieger, *The CIO*, 38-45.

[35] Sydney Fine, *Sit-Down: The General Motors Strike of 1936-1937* (Ann Arbor: University of Michigan Press, 1969); Henry Krause, *The Many and the Few: A Chronicle of the Dynamic Autoworkers*, 2d ed. (Urbana: University of Illinois Press, 1985); Idem., *The UAW, 1934-39: Heroes of Unwritten History* (Urbana: University of Illinois Press, 1993), 205-294; Irving Bernstein, *Turbulent Years: A History of the American Worker, 1933-1941* (Boston: Houghton Mifflin Company, 1970), 318-321.

[36] "Businessman Will Seek to Avert Strike," *Houston Chronicle*, September 14, 1936, p. 1.

[37] Melvyn Dubofsky and Foster Rhea Dulles, *Labor in America: A History*, 8th, ed. (Wheeling: Harlan Davidson, Inc., 2010); Leo Huberman, *The Labor Spy Racket,* (New York: Modern Age Books, 1937).

[38] Henrietta Larson and Kenneth Wiggins Porter, *Humble Oil*, 375.

Twice Through the Glass Ceiling: Sue Birdwell-Alves

By Cynthia Devlin

After the tumult of the 1960s that included the Civil Rights Movement, the Women's Liberation Movement, and the Youth Revolt, women in the South slowly began to step outside the narrow confines of home and family. Young women postponed marriage to enjoy degrees of freedom and self-fulfillment, while some married women reevaluated the status of their marriages or their families' financial stability and thus decided to exercise self-direction and enter the workforce. A few jettisoned their controlling and backward-thinking husbands for the freedom to choose their own destinies. Eventually, these women assisted in breaking the molds that had prevented women from exploring new roles and having careers instead of menial jobs.

One such woman not only established herself as a successful businesswoman in the oil industry, but she also forged a second career in the financial world. Sue Birdwell-Alves began her search for a career in the late 1960s, and in 1974, at the age of forty-five, became the first independent female landman in the traditionally male-driven oil business. She cultivated and courted clients and carved out personal oil royalties while, at the same time, increased the wealth of her customers.

After a successful career as a landman, she revitalized her career and transformed into a stockbroker extraordinaire, garnering the title, "The Legend," by her retirement at seventy-six years of age.[1]

The overt sexism of the time hindered Birdwell-Alves' journey, but she still converted herself from a grits and gravy, white-glove-wearing Southern belle to a suit-wearing, forward-thinking businesswoman of substance, character, and determination. As if overcoming a patriarchy that articulated an Antebellum agenda that prevented the advancement of women in the workplace was not enough, Birdwell-Alves also felt that the women's liberation movement and its unique agenda thwarted her efforts. She insisted that Southern women best made their own path through hard work, longer hours, and acquiring more knowledge than men. According to Birdwell-Alves, southern men projected an

Cynthia Devlin is an adjunct instructor of history at Stephen F. Austin State University.

"Antebellum-Rhett Butler" attitude that sought to keep women barefoot and pregnant, and definitely at home. Birdwell-Alves "knew in her heart" that there were men who believed that qualified women could enter the business world and she simply needed to identify those able to mentor her through the processes necessary to succeed in a man's world. According to Birdwell-Alves, the National Organization for Women, organized by feminist Betty Friedan, promoted a strident, almost militant, agenda that did not much more than disturb the sensibilities and social mores of many Southern women without increasing their chances for success.[2]

Sue Caroline Birdwell (Birdwell-Alves) arrived in the world on April 8, 1929 at Port Arthur, Texas. As the only girl, her brother James Allen Birdwell remembered that their father called her "Sue Baby" and spoiled the young inquisitive child. The world's population stood at a little over two billion in 1929; and by the end of that year, the Great Depression ravaged the nation while businesses and banks in Texas approached paralysis. About twelve million Americans were unemployed by 1932, and people prayed that the economic stimulation and social changes promoted by the Franklin Roosevelt administration would ameliorate and eventually alleviate all the pain and suffering. The Birdwell family fared better than many Americans because most of them had graduated from colleges and universities and worked as professionals. Birdwell-Alves' father, Leroy Birdwell, a graduate of Texas A & M University, worked as an engineer for the Texas Company, the predecessor of Texaco, Incorporated. Alton W. Birdwell, her uncle, served as the first president of Stephen F. Austin State University from September 18, 1923 until 1942. Some females in the family taught school and, as well, some worked outside the home.[3]

Leroy Birdwell moved his family to San Antonio, Texas sometime in 1930 when the Texas Company built a new oil refinery in the area. The headline of the *San Antonio Express* on September 28, 1930 stated, "Better times . . . in store for San Antonio and the rest of the United States." Such a statement defied reality. During the 1930s, the Birdwell family bought and distributed food sacks in their neighborhood to the needy, an art of giving to the community in times of dire need that Birdwell-Alves would apply to her later church and charity work, but lessons that would also provide the foundation for her future in the business world.[4]

While Birdwell-Alves relished her relationships with her male relatives, it was the women who shepherded the young woman into adulthood with solid ideas that a female could select her own destiny through education, drive, and strength of character. Birdwell-Alves' mother, Frances Taylor Birdwell, proved a strong role model for her daughter. Not a traditional housewife and mother, Frances Birdwell acted in the little theatre and performed many deeds of charity for her community. She also directed the activities of the Parent-Teacher's Association as president during Birdwell-Alves' school years. Birdwell-Alves also saw her mother awarded the keys to the city for her work on San Antonio's Riverwalk renewal project in the 1930s. Her aunt, Allie Myrrl Birdwell, also provided the eager-to-learn girl with a fine example of a pioneering woman. Birdwell-Alves noticed with delight when her aunt, a math teacher, published an advanced algebra book in concert with Oscar Miller, the superintendent of schools in San Antonio. She realized at an early age that knowledge truly translated to power. Birdwell-Alves remembered reading together as a family and playing lots of board and card games. She described her childhood as fun but always challenging since her parents expected their children to attend college and to achieve certain goals, especially respectability and competence. Failure to succeed had never been an option for this young and dynamic Texan.[5]

Birdwell-Alves attended high school during World War II. While the city bustled with war-related activities, the Birdwell household celebrated life by hosting air cadets and soldiers for after-church Sunday dinners. Birdwell-Alves stated that "[i]t was common knowledge that my Mama had a big spread of food at 10:30 P.M. every Saturday night." No invitation was needed and, "[a]fter rolling up the rug, we danced," said Birdwell-Alves. They did this because, "Mama knew that it kept teenagers and future soldiers off the streets and out of trouble." During this time period, Lady Bird Johnson purchased KTBC, her first radio station, and the mythical Rosie the Riveter, as portrayed by Norman Rockwell, graced the cover of the *Saturday Evening Post* on May 29, 1943, indicating that women could accomplish men's work. The cover represented the culmination of a government campaign that began in 1942 and had recruited women to the workforce in the name of the "war effort." American women had actually filled necessary roles during all wars, beginning with Abigail Adams, who managed land for her war-engaged husband, John Adams. In the Confederate States of America, women handled plantation activities during the Civil War, and Western women worked homesteads while husbands fought in Indian wars. During the nineteen months of World War I starting in 1917, about one million women went to work as the men went to fight. Those years between the two world wars proved extraordinarily difficult for women who wished to or needed to work. They suffered from workplace discrimination, received low salaries, and often worked in menial jobs with little chance of advancement. Major changes reshaped the workforce when sixteen million men went off to fight in World War II, leaving job vacancies in wartime that nineteen million women eventually filled.[6]

Birdwell-Alves' awareness of women and their roles in the business arena and in the war effort was heightened with her increased exposure to state and national news, as well as with Hollywood's release of pro-American movies that coupled heroics with the warfront scoop. She knew that her observations and reactions to the news, in addition to the non-traditional role model that was her mother, encouraged her to dream without boundaries.

Expectations remained high after the war. Birdwell-Alves graduated from San Antonio's Thomas Jefferson High School in 1947. About that same time, her parents sold the family home and moved to New Jersey, where her father would build a refinery for Texaco. Birdwell-Alves, for the first time in her life, experienced a family void that prompted her to mature quickly as she entered Southwestern University in Georgetown, Texas. During her college years, she guided her sorority as president; and she gained membership in several other honorary organizations. She earned a Bachelor of Science degree in home economics with a minor in history in 1951, joining notable Southwestern graduates such as Texas folklorist J. Frank Dobie and United States Senator John Tower. Twenty-four percent of the degrees awarded in the United States in liberal arts and professional studies in 1950 had gone to women, but in Texas most degreed females worked as secretaries, salesclerks, or teachers.

Home economics, an acceptable major for women during this after-war, pro-domestic transitioning period, had equipped Birdwell-Alves with the skills to run a home and to rear children. Such skills, however, failed to impress most men when she decided to enter the male-dominated work force. Her experience in college, though, provided her the needed organizational skills and time management skills necessary for a productive life. More importantly, Birdwell-Alves honed her exceptional reading skills. Like Birdwell-Alves, many women believed if a woman could run a household efficiently, then she would be able to run a business in the same manner. The study of history at the university provided her a sense of belonging to a larger community, one in which scholars and practitioners promoted the ideas of "American exceptionalism" to counter the Soviet Union's expanded role in the world. Birdwell-Alves believed in capitalism, coupled with democracy, and in the exploits of great American heroes. While seemingly oxymoronic, she remained simultaneously both exceedingly idealistic and completely pragmatic.[7]

For most women, including Birdwell-Alves, the 1950s represented a time when marriage remained the primary lifestyle choice. Women gave up their jobs when the men returned from the war. Despite such a development, 1950 Census data revealed that more women than ever were working, even though most remained housewives and stay-at-home mothers. The proportion of women in the workforce continued to climb yearly, long before women began to organize and clamor for equal rights. Several months after her college graduation, Birdwell-Alves chose marriage to Richard T. Alves, who had been her brother's friend while he attended Texas A & M.

Bogged down in the Korean Conflict (1950-1953), President Harry S. Truman found it necessary under this "police action" to send more troops abroad; and, once more, women took up the slack in the workforce. Thus, Richard T. Alves went to war, and his wife went to work. While he served in the United States Navy, she resided in San Francisco (after living over a year in the Philippines during the Korean War) and worked as a claims clerk for a large insurance company that catered to the trucking industry. She celebrated her employment, finding work outside the home both addictive and intoxicating. The job proved fruitful as her knowledge of business grew extensively. She also enjoyed signing the back of her paycheck and adding it to the bank account. She longed to continue working outside the home after the war ended in 1953; but Richard T. Alves, like so many other Southern-bred men, had other ideas about how a woman should conduct herself.[8]

After leaving the military in 1958, Richard Alves moved the family to Lafayette, Louisiana to work in the oil business. That same year Mary Roebling took the helm as the first woman governor of the American Stock Exchange. Lafayette was home to 586 oil companies in 1959, and the employee payroll of the city was over nine million dollars. Oilmen from Texas and Oklahoma moved their families to the overwhelmingly Catholic, Cajun, and all Democratic city, where folks looked askance at interlopers who spoke English, who did not relish "gators, gumbo, and étouffée," and who acknowledged that America had two major political parties. Because Birdwell-Alves had grown up in the multi-cultural city of San Antonio, she accepted her new environment more easily than some. However, Birdwell-Alves emotionally suffered from the cultural expectations of placing family responsibilities over her own dreams and aspirations. She wondered why she could not have a career and attend to her family obligations as well. After all, men did both. Her frustrations frequently boiled over, but she stifled her desires while promoting her husband's career.[9]

Most young women during the 1950s appeared content to nest in their newly-purchased homes, to rear their children, to wear the new kissable lipstick from chemist Hazel Bishop, and to attend newly organized Tupperware parties; but Birdwell-Alves learned about stocks, land, and wealth. Birdwell-Alves quietly focused dogged attention on the world of finance when she sought to increase the worth of a small amount of stock shares in AT&T and Texaco that she had received as a wedding gift. Not unlike female investor Hetty Green, a Quaker who had amassed a fortune on Wall Street in the mid-to-late 1800s, Birdwell-Alves sought the secrets to financial success.

Combining motherhood with her obsession to learn, she frequented a public library on a quest for knowledge concerning financial matters. She adopted economist and philosopher Adam Smith's idea that "[l] and is the basis of all wealth," and she consumed everything in print written by seminal financial figure Benjamin Graham, who was known as "the father of modern security analysis...and...the founder of the value school of investing." Dismayed to find that women could not open brokerage accounts with financial firms during the 1950s, she insisted that her husband sign the papers on her behalf. An astute self-taught investor, Birdwell-Alves held the gifted stocks through numerous splits, reverse splits, and corporate buyouts, and she relished her financial advantage.[10]

During the 1960s, housewife Birdwell-Alves barely noticed when President John F. Kennedy held the first presidential commission on the status of women, nor did she realize that the world's population had grown to an estimated three billion. However, she did respond negatively to Betty Friedan's *The Feminine Mystique*, dismissing it as "ridiculous rubbish" not founded in logic or reality. Friedan's book undeniably influenced the feminist movement, but to some (such as Birdwell-Alves) her ideas promoted a mythical Amazonian utopia that was unrealistic in theory and in practice. Birdwell-Alves never agreed that female heroines, such as the first stewardesses, as Friedan suggested, represented future role models for women. Stewardesses never directly competed with men whether they were nurses or simply young women seeking adventure. According to Birdwell-Alves, Friedan's references and comparisons remained flawed. By the 1970s, books such as *Coffee, Tea or Me* raised eyebrows with feminists and with Birdwell-Alves because stewardesses morphed into sex goddesses instead of addressing and demonstrating the serious nature of the actual job. The evolution to "sex object" demeaned women and slowed their overall advancement.

When Harvard University admitted the first woman into the Graduate School of Business Administration in 1963, Southern women mainly worked as teachers, nurses, secretaries, and clerks. Birdwell-Alves checked the job want ads for something she could do to fulfill a need to "feel good about her life." Never having learned to type, she felt sick that women had to use their fingers on a bulky machine in order to put bacon on the table when men could use their social skills to make business deals while playing golf at the country club, drinking a beer at a local ice house, or fishing in the Gulf of Mexico. Birdwell-Alves recognized that many Southern women of her generation had simply accepted the traditional idea articulated by Tennessee Williams' character "Big Daddy" Pollitt in his 1955 play *Cat on a Hot Tin Roof*, that women of well-to-do families subjugated their lives to powerful men in order "to be taken care of in the same manner in which they grown accustomed." "Don't worry your pretty little head about it," a common saying by men to women that infuriated some, but also provided comfort to others that someone "was looking after them" did not apply to Birdwell-Alves. She wanted to "look after" herself, and in her eyes "Big Daddies" of the post-World War II era in the urbanizing South were nothing more than reincarnated post-Civil War Bourbons.

Twice Through the Glass Ceiling

Breaking away remained her goal.[11]

Birdwell-Alves' experience, as with so many women of her generation in the South, stemmed from her volunteer work through her church and other community services. Her summers were spent teaching Vacation Bible School and organizing family gatherings. She had reared her children well and had sent them off to college. She soon found herself grappling with the idea of divorce because of the social, moral, and religious implications; and she consulted trusted family members and close friends about her dilemma. After resolving the emotional conflict between the need to exercise her own personal freedom and the idea that she should remain married out of a sense of tradition, she traded her Antebellum-thinking husband for a chance to succeed in the business world. At forty-five years of age and without health insurance, the newly divorced and somewhat physically frail Birdwell-Alves charged ahead with her dreams. She was not alone. Twenty million women went to work between 1975 and 1990, some seeking career opportunities, while others simply needed the money. Birdwell-Alves, unlike most of the women entering the workplace, did not need the money because throughout the 1960s she earned dividends from her stock investments.

Birdwell-Alves was far from the stereotypical women's rights pioneer of the 1960s and 1970s. She realized that most women of her generation had not finished college and some had never gone at all; thus, they would find careers closed to them due to experience or education requirements. As a traditionalist she felt uneasy about the social chaos of the time, and the headlines that called the Vietnam War endless and not winnable probably dismayed her. Never having been prejudiced, she applauded the Civil Rights Movement and, no doubt, supported the idea of feminine equality. Women's rights issues to her, however, did not include the need or right to burn bras, to live in communes, or to smoke marijuana. Jane Fonda's trip to support the North Vietnamese violated her closely held conservative philosophy, and her values very often conflicted with the leaders of the "women's movment." Nevertheless, she remained an active citizen who voted and assisted the less fortunate; but she also moved forward with her personal goals in this time of social upheaval.[12]

By the early 1970s, Birdwell-Alves had established herself as the unofficial "go-to-woman" for many of her female friends who needed expertise on how best to manage their money. She had met most of these women through her church and her numerous charities,;and when some became widows, Birdwell-Alves often became an advisor to prevent them from financial ruin. Few knew how to balance a checkbook; how to budget for household expenses; or, much less, how to invest money and have that investment furnish a financial future. Birdwell-Alves urged her friends to assume the economic responsibility necessary to provide a good life for themselves and their children without a husband guiding the way. She noted that one widow simply spent the life insurance money until "precious little remained", and it barely fed her and the children while the woman learned to type and find employment. She actively promoted the idea of education and encouraged women to go to college and earn degrees that would provide them an entrée into the job market.[13]

While companies such as Motorola and Deloitte and Touche formulated and enhanced programs for the promotion of women into lower-level management, oil companies and service companies in the South seldom considered women qualified for promotion. Birdwell-Alves noted that men without college degrees often moved up the ladder in the oil business, whereas a female secretary with the same high school degree remained forever a secretary with few raises and no pension. The Equal Pay Act of 1963 and the Civil Rights Act of 1964 prevented discriminatory practices in pay and promotion; however, Birdwell-Alves noted a prevailing antiquated attitude that considered the ideal woman to be "family oriented, not business oriented." Complaints to the boss usually meant a dismissal from the job. She wanted such a mindset changed.[14]

Regardless of the obstacles, Birdwell-Alves decided on a career as an oil landman. Although a few women landmen during this time worked for large oil companies, such as Donna Gustafson of Chevron, who was jokingly referred to in a local Plano newsletter as a "landlady," Birdwell-Alves entered the business world in 1974 as the first independent female landman. Ironically, while she could work as a landman, according to Louisiana law of the time she could not serve on a jury, a discriminatory barrier that did not end until 1975 with the *Taylor v. Louisiana* decision by the United States Supreme Court. She secured her position as a landman through a network of contacts she had met and cultivated through her charitable efforts. She chose the oil industry because Lafayette had been an oil center since the 1950s and was dedicated to the growth of the industry. The oil business during the 1970s remained difficult due to Middle Eastern oil embargoes; oil shortages; and, according to many in the industry, the formation of the Department of Energy in October, 1977. The purpose of this government agency was the following:

> The Department provided the framework for a comprehensive and balanced national energy plan by coordinating and administering the energy functions of the federal government. The Department undertook responsibility for long-term, high-risk research and development of energy technology, federal power marketing, energy conservation, the nuclear weapons program, energy regulatory programs, and a central energy data collection and analysis program.

Texan Eddie Chiles of the Western Company of North America became an unofficial spokesperson for oil-related companies upset with federal government policies and with government overspending during the 1970s. His television ads, radio ads, and automobile bumper stickers in Texas, Oklahoma, and Louisiana expressed the opinions of many in the oil producing states: "Let the Yankee bastards freeze in the dark" and "If you don't have an oil well... get one." Birdwell-Alves remained undaunted and, as she noted, "I worked in the [oil] business because that was where the money was." She instinctively knew that without the help of oilmen the doors would remain closed.[15]

One who gave her help was Robert G. Furse, Sr., a West Texas oilman whose family hobnobbed with George Herbert Walker Bush's family at Kennebunkport, Maine. Furse, a Yale graduate and a past president of the Lafayette Petroleum Landmen's Association, was also a leader of the International Association of Petroleum Landmen. He lived in Birdwell-Alves' neighborhood. After some joint discussions, he assisted her with her career objectives, and he obtained the all-important health insurance provided by a group policy through the international association. Furse, as Birdwell-Alves stated, "made it happen." Without a mentor her foray into the oil business would have easily failed; mentoring proved crucial to her success as a newcomer to the industry, and Furse assisted her in the development of a business plan and instructed her as to the execution of that plan. He also coached her in the intricacies of starting and running your own business. As a mentee, Birdwell-Alves clarified her goals, thought through her problems, and graciously demanded feedback from Furse. When doubts and fears crept through her mind during the wee hours of the night, she knew that her mentor would provide encouragement at their next meeting.[16]

Birdwell-Alves tapped her male contacts and finessed her way through the gender differences in order to convert such folks to clients. At first, she experienced some uneasiness from those who did not know her, but won over most; and they willingly assisted her. Some men refused to speak with her and others "told her off"; some, in vivid language, suggested that she go home and "fry up" something. Instead, she steeled her emotions, sutured her wounds, and fertilized her dreams as she transformed herself into a landman.

The term "landman" most likely originated with the British Royal Navy during the eighteenth century at a time when sailors referred to a seaman who had less than one year's experience as a "landman." Later, this informal assessment changed to a formal ranking. Presently, the term "landman" refers to those, both male and female, who "do negotiations and title research work for oil and mining companies." Birdwell-Alves negotiated various pathways to her success by turning obstacles into open doors. Since, as a female, she could not belong to the Petroleum Club of Lafayette, she had to garner an invitation. Because she was never invited on deep-sea fishing trips with the area oilmen, she found a way to meet them at local restaurants or to "corner them" after church. Oilmen played golf, but females could not join country clubs at the time. Instead, Birdwell-Alves knew where the men met for morning coffee; and she sat at the counter. She remained positive and relentless in her pursuit of success.[17]

Nineteen parishes define the state of Louisiana, and Birdwell-Alves combed through old land records in five of them in attempts to locate leasable land with the potential of production for her clients. Some landmen remained skeptical that she had the skills to maneuver the convoluted land records of a state whose Spanish- and French-inspired legal title system was arcane and obscure, to say the least. Ever diligent, Birdwell-Alves worked at learning the necessary processes that serviced her clients well. She studied and learned how to read old maps in dusty and dimly lit parish courthouses. Louisiana land records date to the initial French occupation from the years 1698 to 1763 and from the takeover by the Spanish in 1763 until Spain returned the territory to France in 1803. France owned Louisiana for about twenty days before Napoleon Bonaparte sold it to the United States.[18]

Louisiana is a federal-land state, meaning that lands were generally acquired from foreign sovereigns and then transferred to the United States government. After the famous Louisiana Purchase, owners of land had to prove their ownership to the United States, and those land recordings are now contained within what is known as "The Superior Council Records." While landmen today can access those files on microfilm at Tulane University in New Orleans, Birdwell-Alves patiently dug through such records in a pre-computer world, where analytical and critical thinking skills proved indispensable. Because Louisiana retained the "Napoleonic Code of Law," landmen accessed records that contained the husband's and wife's names and those of all of the heirs who happened to be living at the time of death of either spouse as directed by that code. Most oil company landmen tapped the legal minds of lawyers for an understanding of French law and the nuances and anomalies that set it apart from the common English law of the other forty-nine states. Birdwell-Alves sought advice from Lafayette oil and gas attorney S. K. Hartley, and he proved a strong mentor for the novice landman. He also knew researchers who would assist her with land records. Birdwell-Alves' overall successes rested not only on her continuing educational endeavors and her attendance at relevant seminars, but on her development of these strong personal relationships.[19]

After making inroads into the landman business, Birdwell-Alves' male clients frequently escorted her to the Petroleum Club in Lafayette. These men were members, and they bought her meals. Many times she attempted to pay, but the club refused to accept her money. Dow Chemical Company conducted business at the club, and when one of their in-house female landmen was not allowed inside, they supported the woman in a lawsuit. Dow Chemical won the suit and management requested that Birdwell-Alves become one of the first female members. In a short and swift proclamation, she stated, "No, I don't need you now." As with the tenor of the times, many service clubs, such as Rotary International, the Jaycees, the Kiwanis, and the Lions, did not permit women to join. Finally, in the 1984 case *Roberts v. U.S. Jaycees, 468 U.S. 609* (1984), the Supreme Court outlawed sex discrimination in membership policies of organizations, opening many previously all-male organizations to women. Following the decision, Birdwell-Alves, who had been asked to address, according to her own words, "some pretty powerful groups," at some of these clubs, declined a 1988 invitation to join the Rotary International Club, but accepted membership in 1990 as the third woman to become a Rotarian in Lafayette. Moreover, Birdwell-Alves became the first woman member of the Lafayette Association of Petroleum Landmen. She later joined by invitation many local and national service organizations, including several financial committees and directorships of the Asbury Methodist Church. She assisted many of these organizations with financial advice on how best to manage their money and to remain solvent.[20]

An opportunity next arose that permitted Birdwell-Alves to fulfill her adult dream of becoming a stockbroker. She saw an ad in the local paper about a test that would be given on a certain day and at a specific time for a financial position. She tested for the position, not knowing the name of the company that posted the potential job. Shortly thereafter, in 1984, Birdwell-Alves became assistant trader at Howard Weil Lahouisse & Friedricks, a financial firm headquartered in New Orleans. Management took a gamble on her, and the company manager never failed to remind her that she had absolutely no financial background.

Social and cultural pressures confronted working women concerning their wardrobe choices and their physical appearances during the 1970s and through the 1980s. Birdwell-Alves strongly believed that the Women's Movement emphasized "dress" over substance in the struggle to compete with men in the workforce. She had no intentions of conforming to the standards articulated by women's magazines. Designers such as Diane Von Furstenberg introduced what became known as a career woman's staple, a simple jersey knit wrap dress. The wrap dress seemed conservative at a time when Southwest Airlines introduced flight attendants in "hot pants" and boots. Diane Keaton, in the 1977 movie *Annie Hall*, introduced and accelerated the men's wear look for women in the workforce. By the late 1970s and early 1980s, many women seeking to move up in their careers wore ties to work with men-styled shirts and houndstooth patterned suits in an attempt to compete with men for promotions. Seeing no need to dress as a man, Birdwell-Alves purchased beautifully tailored feminine suits and topped them with butterfly broaches and pretty necklaces. She intended to win in the workforce based on her business acumen, rather than attire. One of the reasons for her confidence certainly stemmed from her successes as a landman.[21]

Management quickly realized that the savvy lady knew the ins-and-outs of stock and bonds. They insisted Birdwell-Alves become a registered broker, and she passed the test the first go-around, becoming the company's very first female stock trader. In order to become an investment adviser, all persons must receive a series 66 license, issued by the Financial Industry Regulatory Authority (FINRA). Then, in order to sell stocks and other securities, all persons must obtain a series 7 license, also issued by the FINRA. A series 7 license authorized Birdwell-Alves to sell stocks, bonds, certificates of deposit, mutual funds, commodities, and limited partnerships. She earned both licenses. However, she needed to amass a certain amount of money "under management" within ninety days or "she was out." Such a challenge provided her with the opportunity to use the great connections she had nurtured during her landman career. She called many of her former clients and asked for their business. Roustabouts, petroleum engineers, wildcatters, and oil executives brought their money to her because they trusted her judgment, and they had no qualms about placing their financial futures in her hands. She immediately went to work maximizing their portfolios; and after the fiscal quarter closed, the profits exceeded the expectations of management and that of her clients. As time passed, the leadership of the company treated her as a "seasoned pro and with respect."[22]

Legg Mason, Wood, Walker, Inc. purchased Howard Weil in 1986, and during the 1987 stock market drop of five hundred points in one day, chaos ensued at the company. Many brokers resigned under pressure. Management promoted Birdwell-Alves to the position of manager, and she assumed the duties of federal compliance and contended that she happened "to be in the right place at the right time." Birdwell-Alves had courted relationships with the members of the board of directors and with upper management, and she had impressed them with her financial acumen. James W. Brinkley, the Chief Executive Officer of

Legg Mason, became her new mentor.[23]

Legg Mason formed a team of financial advisors in 1996 that enhanced and expanded the efforts of Birdwell-Alves, who had amassed huge assets for the company, as well as a strong client base. She had made it in a man's world; the glass ceiling crashed, and she was near the top: "The glass ceiling is a theory that attempts to explain why women do not advance into the uppermost professional and managerial jobs in business." The belief remains strong that the rise of women entrepreneurs stemmed from their inability to move forward in traditional companies. Birdwell-Alves had formed her own business in 1974, and by 1996 she had moved forward in a traditional company. She had accomplished two major goals by becoming not only an independent entrepreneur, but a corporate team player as well. Her financial partners included Glen Raxsdale and Randy Landry, both of whom she assisted as they progressed in the financial industry. She mentored many men and women, and older men with younger wives came to Birdwell-Alves because she had the reputation of taking care of widows and ensuring their financial security.[24]

So serious was Birdwell-Alves about educating women on financial matters that she agreed in 1991 to address, without compensation, the Association of Women in Management Fall Conference in Denver, Colorado. This small group of women originated at Eastern Airlines; and after the company filed for bankruptcy in 1989, Continental Airlines hired many of them. They continued the association with educational seminars; however, the fall conference never took place because Continental filed for bankruptcy in December of 1990. Birdwell-Alves provided complimentary advice to several of these women, even after the cancellation. No woman, according to Birdwell-Alves, should depend on a man for her complete financial support. She spent hours assisting women whose finances were tangled to the point that their financial solvency remained dubious. Particularly worried about elderly women, Birdwell-Alves created financial plans so these ladies could avoid becoming dependent on family members for their survival: "The difference between an old woman and an elderly lady—so goes the old saying—is money." Until 2007, she provided complimentary financial advice to all the widows who attended her brother's church in Katy, Texas. By the end of her career, Birdwell-Alves had clients as far away as Indonesia and from all over the oil-producing states. She continued attending seminars and absorbing everything possible about all things financial. Moreover, Birdwell-Alves insisted that her clients learn about the market and read consequential financial material.[25]

Legg Mason, a Baltimore, Maryland-based company, grew rapidly in Lafayette and was eventually acquired by Citigroup, Smith Barney in December of 2005. In May 2007 her original mentor at Legg Mason and presently the vice-chairman of Smith Barney Private Client Group, James W. Brinkley, introduced Birdwell-Alves as a shining star and acknowledged their long friendship at a Smith-Barney client-broker luncheon in Lafayette. She relished the mention of her new title, "The Legend."[26]

Birdwell-Alves eventually retired to conduct a personal battle against cancer. Her only son had become ill and passed away in 1996, but she continued a close and strong relationship with her brother, her daughter, and her grandchildren, whom she insisted go to college and "make something out of themselves." They did, and Birdwell-Alves glowed with pride over her granddaughters' accomplishments. She fought her cancer as she had all the obstacles placed in front of her by economic, social, and cultural pressures during her lifetime. Sue Caroline Birdwell-Alves died March 31, 2008. A celebration of her life was conducted at the Asbury United Methodist Church in Lafayette, Louisiana, on April 5, 2008. One of her favorite quotes was from Isaiah 40:31: "They shall mount up with wings like eagles, they shall walk and not be weary, they shall run and not faint." [27]

Birdwell-Alves believed that a woman of her generation "had to work harder than a man and she must know more." Glass ceilings had crashed around her because she had remained self-motivated, she had good role models, she had graduated from college, she had worked during wartime, she had benefited from court cases and legislation meant to assist women, and she had dared to enter a male-dominated sphere of business by seeking the help of good, strong male mentors willing to assist her. Proactively setting her strategies for success, Birdwell-Alves secured her future through processes that enabled her to mentor, to teach, and to tutor a younger generation, whose business sojourns proved less daunting because of her ability to pass that knowledge and experience forward in a society that previously had shown more deference to men than women. By dismissing the image of Scarlet O'Hara, who exercised feminine wiles in order to survive, Birdwell-

Alves employed brainpower and her love of learning to win in a man's world during an age of urbanization and hyper-consumerism. Unlike the main character in Sloan Wilson's *The Man in the Gray Flannel Suit*, she had no ruminations about her decision to earn money and to be happy in her job because her children were grown. However, for many women and men, that quandary of how best to balance family obligations and career mandates still weighs heavily on their minds. Birdwell-Alves enjoyed the money provided by her labor; however, she never believed it necessary to "show off", she drove a twelve-year-old Oldsmobile in a time when two stockbrokers who reported to her drove those ubiquitous BMWs popular with the successful set. Her money went to scholarship funds and to charities of her choice. Birdwell-Alves' immediate and extended family members provided strength, encouragement, and praise—all needed and desired elements of her successes. In particular, her brother James Birdwell "sang her praises" and remained her muse until her death. As she had written in a personal letter, "I think I led a very charmed life. Weren't I blessed?" Yes, but she was also smart and quite determined to crash through that glass ceiling not only once, but twice.[28]

(Endnotes)

[1] Sue Birdwell-Alves, interview by Cynthia M. Devlin, 5 July 2007; AAPL – American Association of Professional Landmen, <http://www.landman.org> (20 February 2007).

[2] Birdwell-Alves interview.

[3] Office of Public Affairs. "About SFA," 7 September 2007, <http://www.2.sfasu.edu/publicaffairs/SFA-about.html>; James Birdwell, interview by Cynthia M. Devlin, 17 September 2007.

[4] Birdwell-Alves interview; Birdwell interview; "Repatriation in San Antonio," <http://www.repatriationsanantoniocolfa.etsa.edu> (20 February 2007); Randolph Air Force Base, <http://www.randolph.af.mil/library/factsheet> (20 February 2007); Carol Krismann, *Encyclopedia of American Women in Business: From Colonial Times to the Present*, Vol. 2 (Westport, CT: Greenwood Press, 2005), 476.

[5] Birdwell-Alves interview; Birdwell interview; "San Antonio

Riverwalk History," <http://www.sanantonioriverwalk.com/history.html> (6 July 2007).

[6] Carol Krismann, *Encyclopedia of American Women in Business: From Colonial Times to the Present*, Vol. 1 (Westport, CT: Greenwood Press, 2005), xxx, xxix; Birdwell-Alves interview; "OCS Oral History Project," Department of History & Geography, University of Louisiana at Lafayette, <http://www.louisiana.edu/academic/liberal> (10 July 2007).

[7] "John Tower Biography," < http://www.smu.edu.twer/biography> (18 October 2007); "J. Frank Dobie," <http://www.library.txstate.edu/swwc/exhibit.dobie> (18 October 2007); Birdwell-Alves interview; Robert A. Calvert, Arnoldo DeLeón, and Gregg Cantrell, *The History of Texas*, 3rd ed. (Wheeling, Illinois: Harlan Davidson, Inc., 2002), 416.

[8] Birdwell-Alves interview; Birdwell interview. Stephanie Coontz, *The Way We Never Were: American Families and the Nostalgia Trap* (New York: BasicBooks, Inc., 1992) 157-159.

[9] Virginia Drachman, *Enterprising Women: 250 Years of American Business* (Chapel Hill, NC: The University of North Carolina Press) 70-73; Birdwell-Alves interview; "Benjamin Graham," <http://www.bufferstock.org/graham.htm> (10 July 2007).

[10] Dorothy P. Moore and E. Holly Buttner, *Women Entrepreneurs: Moving Beyond the Glass Ceiling* (Thousand Oaks, CA: Sage Publications, 1997) 1; Birdwell-Alves interview; Krismann, Vol. 1, xxix.

[11] Betty Friedan, *The Feminine Mystique* (New York: W. W. Norton and Co., 1963) 40-41; Birdwell-Alves interview; Trudy Baker and Rachel Jones, *Coffee, Tea or Me* (New York: Bantum Books, 1974), 140; Bret Harvey, *The Fifties: A Women's Oral History* (New York: Harper Collins, 1993) 140.

[12] Birdwell-Alves interview; "Legacy '98: Detailed Timeline," <http://www.legacy98.org.timeline.html> (14 July 2007).

[13] Birdwell-Alves interview.

[14] Birdwell-Alves interview; "Women In Business," <http://www.referenceforbusiness.com/enclycopedia/Val-Z?Women-in-Business.html> (21 February 2007).

[15] Birdwell-Alves interview; "Donna Gustason," Professional Landmen's Association of New Orleans <http://www.planoweek.org/1970.asp> (14 July 2007); Taylor v Louisiana, 419 U.S. 522 (1975), Cornell University Law School; Mark Singer, *Funny Money* (New York: Knopf, 1985) 21; "Origins & Evolutions of the Department of Energy," Department of Energy---History. <http://www.energy.gov./abouthistory.htm> (15 August 2010); "Mad Eddie," <http://www.time.com/tim/printout/).8816951478.00html> (1 August 2007).

[16] Krismann, Vol 2, 375; Birdwell-Alves interview; "History of Landmen," <http://www.landmentechnology.infomine.com> (21 February 2007).

[17] Birdwell-Alves interview; Louisiana Public Records Information, <http://www.publicrecordsinfo.com/public_records/Louisiana_public_records.htm> (14 July 2007).

[18] Birdwell-Alves interview; Thomas A. Bailey, *The American Pageant: A History of the Republic*, 5th ed. (Lexington, MA: D.C. Heath and Company, 1975) 200-201.

[19] Birdwell-Alves interview; "Louisiana Genealogy," <http://www.accessmylibrary.com/comsite5/bin/pdinventory.pl?page=s...ITM&item_id=0286-7107144> (14 July 2007).

[20] "United Methodist Foundation of Louisiana," s.v. leadership http://www.umf.org/default.asp?id=14 (20 February 2007); Birdwell-Alves interview.

[21] Robin D. Givhan, "Diane Von Furstenberg Caters to the Masses---and Their Money," *Washington Post*, 5 January 1966; "Hot Pants, Southwest Airlines, <http://www.time.com/time/2003/flight/fashion4.html> (13 August 2010).

[22] Birdwell-Alves interview.

[23] Birdwell-Alves interview.

[24] Birdwell-Alves interview.

[25] Birdwell-Alves interview; Citigroup/SmithBarney, "James W.

Brinkley Biography," document 190880: FCM7008; Mary Elizabeth Schlayer and Marilyn Cooley, *How to Be a Financially Secure Woman* (New York: Rawson Associates Publishers, Inc., 1978), 2; The Association of Women in Management at Eastern Airlines promoted the idea that women mentoring women was the best way to move up the business ladder during the 1980s and 1990s. Eastern Airlines employed approximately 18,000 employees. Approximately sixty women in management registered for the seminar held in Miami in 1990. Forty-six women registered for the Feb. 26, 1991 meeting in Houston. Eastern Airlines filed for bankruptcy March 9, 1989 and was completely liquidated in 1991. The fall 1991 meeting that Birdwell-Alves was scheduled to address in Denver was canceled because Continental Airlines filed for bankruptcy.

[26] Birdwell-Alves interview.

[27] Birdwell-Alves interview, Birdwell-Alves obituary.

[28] Birdwell-Alves interview; Sue Birdwell-Alves, handwritten letter to Cynthia Devlin, 3 September 2007, Devlin personal papers; Birdwell interview.

Narrative of Neglect: Texas Prisons for Men

By J. Keith Price and Susan Coleman

Prisons, like the prisoners themselves, are often "[b]anished from everyday sight, they exist in a shadow world that only dimly enters [the public's] awareness."[1] During the 181 years of the Texas prison system's existence, both the people and the policymakers have adhered to such a maxim. The hallmarks of the Texas correctional policy—the initial reluctance to establish prisons and chronic lack of oversight, coupled with the state's well-documented fiscally conservative approach to social programs—have created decades of neglect, leading to what even Texas officials themselves have acknowledged as some of the worst prisons in the nation.[2]

The policy is a product of the state's political culture, the Puritan work ethic, the Calvinistic belief in discipline, and a hint of Social Darwinism. Daniel J. Elazar's classic model identified the political culture of Texas as individualistic-traditionalistic. Texans generally view government as "being instituted for strictly utilitarian reasons" with the effect that "public officials are normally not willing to initiate new programs or open up new areas of government activity on their own recognizance,"[3] which explains Texas' long reluctance to establish a prison system and the aversion of policymakers to intercede in prison operations to end the abuse of inmates and corruption of the system. That reluctance squares with one of Elazar's cultural indicators that government officials are "willing to [act] only when they perceive an overwhelming public demand for them to act."[4]

While neglect by the state has been the dominant paradigm for Texas prisons, there have been brief spates of reform—internally and externally generated. Outside reformers, such as coalitions of church groups and related organizations, media investigations, and the courts through inmate-initiated litigation, have spurred most changes in the system. Other reformers have included influential, often charismatic,

J. Keith Price is an associate professor of Criminal Justice and Sociology at West Texas A&M University and spent thirty years employed with the Texas prison system. Susan Coleman is an attorney and Director of the Criminal Justice Program at West Texas A&M University.

Narrative of Neglect: Texas Prisons for Men

Historical Eras of the Texas Prison System

Era	Years
Early Beginnings	1829 - 1870
The Convict Lease System	1871 - 1910
Prison Farms	1910 - 1947
The Progressive Era	1948 - 1979
Ruiz Reform	1979 - 1992
Prison Bureaucracy	1992 - Present

prison administrators. Like the state itself, the prison system has a rich and textured history.

Spain and then Mexico established the first governmental entities in Texas, but neither the Spanish nor the Mexican governments created a penal institution in its Texas colony.[5] Texas was sparsely populated because many were unwilling to relocate to the territory and face the many challenges that were part of life on the frontier. However, a nearby pool of available immigrants, the independent and opportunistic Americans, was willing to dwell in this inhospitable land. Stephen F. Austin and other *empresarios* who received land grants to bring in new settlers screened the newcomers, but many persons of questionable character entered the Texas territory.[6] Law enforcement, and by extension corrections, was uneven, uncertain, and rough, and lawlessness was rampant. Punishment was often by means of public whipping or even by hanging.

The Congress of *Coahuila y Tejas* passed a resolution in 1829 to establish the first prison in Texas.[7] A private contractor was to build and finance the prison, with labor provided by territorial convicts. He would also be required to train and supervise all prisoners whose sentences included forced labor. If a prisoner worked hard and successfully completed his sentence, he would be sent to the territorial town of his choice upon his release. No contractors responded to this economic opportunity, and the resolution passed into history. The territory of Texas thus remained without a prison.[8]

Following a brief revolution in 1836, Texas became an independent republic. Under Republic law, county jails housed all prisoners. An early example of the county jail system was San Augustine County, where public subscription built the jail. The first Congress appropriated $15,000 under the "Sheriffs – Fees – Keeping Prisoners Act" to reimburse the counties for the prisoners' upkeep, but sheriffs felt funding failed to meet the Republic's responsibility. One sheriff, Henry M. Smith of Galveston County, billed the Republic $864.63 for his expenditures on national prisoners. Congress debated legislation in 1841 to establish a national prison system, but the proposal failed.[9]

A second attempt to pass a penitentiary act in 1842 also died, iterating the pattern of neglect.[10] In December 1845, the Republic of Texas ceased to exist, and Texas became the twenty-eighth state of the United States of America.

One of the first topics of business for the new state was to address the issue of prisons; the First Legislature passed a penitentiary act in May 1846. Once again, Texas constructed no prison as the outbreak of the Mexican War the same year delayed implementation. After the war, the legislature once more tackled the issue of a penitentiary. It passed legislation declaring that "the new prison would be a place where inmates would be forced to abide by strict rules of behavior and discipline and would work so as not to be a burden on the state's taxpayers."[11] The Act authorized the governor to appoint three commissioners who were, in turn, to select a site for the state's first prison and to hire a superintendent to manage the institution. The statute provided that the prison should be located in a healthy climate and be near a navigable body of water for transportation of convict-made goods to market. The chosen location should contain no more than one hundred acres and could cost no more than five dollars an acre.[12]

The commissioners selected Huntsville, in Walker County, as the site for the new prison. The commissioners purchased 4.8 acres of land at the rate of $22 per acre for the actual site and an additional tract of heavily-forested land for $470 to support the construction. "The reasons for the choice of Huntsville remain a mystery. That the town was home to Sam Houston and other notable figures in early Texas [including Commissioner William Palmer] possibly played a part. Similarly, local support for the institution, demonstrated by the gifts of rock and timber, likely also had a favorable influence on the committee members."[13] Community support and continued political clout contributed to the location of new prisons in close proximity to Huntsville until the building explosion in the 1990s. The Commission hired noted Austin architect Abner H. Cook to design the prison, to supervise the construction crews, and to manage the new penitentiary. Construction began on August 5, 1848.[14]

More than one hundred sixty years after the first settlers arrived and forty years after the first legislation was introduced, policymakers finally met their obligation to insure public safety by removing the worst lawbreakers from society and imprisoning them. The Texas State Penitentiary at Huntsville opened on October 1, 1849. The first prisoner was a convicted horse thief. The penitentiary housed three convicts by the end of 1849, and initially the population grew relatively slowly (seventy-five by 1855). However, it quickly became obvious that the public and their elected representatives were no more eager to financially support the prison than they were to create it initially.[15]

The legislature, at the behest of Governor Peter H. Bell in 1853, had crafted a partial solution—the establishment of a cotton and woolen mill within the prison walls. The income would offset the costs of the prison operations while also providing work for inmates.[16] "During the Civil War the penitentiary sold more than two million yards of cotton and nearly 300,000 yards of wool to both civilians and the government of the Confederate States of America. Wartime production made a profit of $800,000."[17] The prison also supported the Confederacy by housing Union prisoners of war. One of these, the ship's carpenter from a federal vessel captured at Galveston, built the coffin of the prisoners' frequent visitor, Sam Houston, who had left his office as governor of Texas rather

47

than support secession.[18]

The State Penitentiary at Huntsville, commonly known as "The Walls," was the only prison in the eleven Confederate states that survived the war intact.[19] Like other prisons of the era, conditions at The Walls were grim. Conditions were unsanitary, and diseases spread rapidly. The food was poor and sparse. Discipline was carried out at the unfettered discretion of the guards and often included whipping and other forms of corporal punishment. Inmates could be assigned to the "dark cell," a dank, dark, filthy cell without ventilation or light, opportunities for hygiene, or running water, and only bread and water as a diet.[20] Incarceration at The Walls amounted to "banishment from civilized society to a dark and evil world completely alien to the free world."[21]

By the end of the Civil War, the number of convicts had increased from 146 to 264, and that number rapidly rose as lawlessness increased during the chaos of Reconstruction. The former Confederate state was in dire financial straits and had little money and less inclination to deal with convicts or their care. The legislature created a five-member Board of Public Labor in 1866 to administer the penitentiary, which consisted of the governor, secretary of state, comptroller, attorney general, and the state treasurer. The new Board acted immediately to lease one hundred prisoners to the Airliner Railroad and one hundred fifty prisoners to the Brazos Branch Railroad as laborers laying railroad track. The convict lease system had begun.[22]

The convict lease system presented an attractive solution to the cash-strapped state in the midst of Reconstruction. Ignored was the inherent conflict between the contractors who wanted to maximize their profits and minimize their labor costs and the state that wanted prisoners to have adequate food, clothing, and shelter. Because of the mistreatment of prisoners and the administrative difficulties, the first contracts were abandoned and the inmates returned to the prison.

The governor and legislature abdicated their responsibility for the prison operations and the welfare of the inmates in 1871 by leasing the entire prison system to Ward Dewey and Company, a well-regarded and successful business venture in Galveston. The lease required the contractor to house, secure, and care for all prisoners under the control of the company. The lease fee was first set at $5,000, then $10,000, and finally $20,000 per year. Initially, the contractual arrangements appeared successful. However, the company began to have financial difficulties, and the state was forced to repossess the penitentiary in 1877.[23]

The state subsequently negotiated a lease with Ed Cunningham and L. A. Ellis, landowners from the south and west of Houston, who utilized convict labor on their large agricultural holdings and also subleased the inmates to other landowners, small industries, and railroads. Cunningham and Ellis earned substantial profits from the leases, which convinced the legislature that prison labor was profitable, so the state resumed control of the prison system in 1883.[24]

Convicts also worked on state projects, such as building the state capitol in Austin. Between 1885 and 1887, approximately five hundred prisoners quarried granite and limestone or worked on the construction site. The International Association of Granite Cutters boycotted the job in protest of the use of convict labor in competition with free labor, so stone cutters from Scotland arrived to complete the work. Selected inmates were also trained to cut stone.[25] Prisoners at the Rusk Penitentiary, constructed to help develop iron-ore deposits in East Texas, manufactured the building's ornate interior cast-iron features in its twenty-five-ton blast furnace. To transport the stone from the quarry and the cast iron from the foundry to Austin, the inmates constructed railroads. They also built the Texas State Railroad from Rusk to Palestine between 1893 and 1909, and the prison system owned the line until 1921.[26]

Convicts assigned to state projects existed in the same dismal, cruel, and inhumane conditions as those leased to private entities. Self-mutilation, such as cutting off one's fingers or toes or otherwise injuring oneself to avoid the lease work, was commonplace, as was suicide. Texas inmates were generally not employed on roads, as was the custom in other southern states but, instead, worked in rural areas on farms, in mining operations, and in wood camps, essentially isolated from the public (and media) view. White and Hispanic inmates often went to the lumber camps, the mines, and the railroads while the state sent black inmates to farms, where they cut sugarcane, picked cotton, and worked in the fields. Inmates considered a high risk for escape in the fields were put into "the spur," an iron ankle band with "spurs" pointing upward that would interfere with an inmate's running, while others toiled with an iron two and a half pound ball and chain attached. Other punishments included hanging by the wrists—from singletrees, from block and tackles, from windows, from ladders on cotton trailers—with toes barely touching the ground or in a squatting position for hours, generally in public areas, such as hallways, so that other inmates could observe. A similar practice that continued until the 1970s was prisoners being forced to stand on a barrel or some variation (milk cartons, coke bottles, oil drums) all night with the intent of causing severe leg cramps. If the inmate fell or stepped off, the time started again.[27] In a single year, 1876, with a prison population of approximately 1700, there were sixty-two deaths recorded and 382 escapes.[28]

Even as the system provided revenue for the struggling state, tales of the abuse of prisoners filtered out to the general public. An investigative report by the *San Antonio Express* revealed a long history of prisoner abuse, neglect, and hellish living conditions. It also documented mismanagement and corruption on the part of public officials. The report and a special session of the legislature ended the convict lease system in 1910.[29]

Offsetting the darkness, to a limited degree, of this period of Texas corrections was the administration of Superintendent Thomas Goree. Goree, a lawyer, initiated basic education classes taught by fellow inmates and gathered a library of several thousand volumes for prisoner use. For the first time, Texas' prisons employed a classification scheme when officials mandated that first-time and non-violent offenders, as well as vulnerable inmates, be segregated from more hardcore and experienced criminals. Goree also advocated the use of indeterminate sentencing and the use of "good time", which inmates would earn by engaging in good behavior, by taking advantage of educational programs, and, of course, by working. Prison administrators of the time served at the pleasure of the governor, and Goree was not reappointed in 1893 by Governor James Hogg because he had not supported Hogg's candidacy.[30]

The end of the convict lease system deprived the state of income, but it had shown prison officials and others that agricultural work was an ideal form of labor for unskilled prisoners.[31] The Civil War had devastated Texas' economy. Many plantation owners sold their lands due to the end of slavery or, like small landowners, lost property to bank foreclosures, high taxes, low prices for crops, the depletion of livestock herds, lack of available and cheap labor, and the inability to move their products to market because the means of transportation had been destroyed.[32] The state, with a ready supply of free labor, saw this as an opportunity to cheaply amass substantial amounts of land, on which they essentially continued the plantation system, one staffed by inmates rather than slaves.

The state acquired the first farms, the Central Farm and the W.F. Ramsey I Farm, in 1908 amid discussions that the convict lease system should be ended.[33] In two waves, the state purchased the Wynne, Harlem, Clemens, Imperial, Ramsey, Darrington, Retrieve, Blue Ridge, Eastham, and Shaw Farms. The prison farms occupied over 81,000 acres by 1921. The prison had entered the era of state-owned, convict-worked agricultural programs.[34]

The prison farm era continued the brutality of the convict lease period. Whippings persisted as did the use of the "bat," a twenty-four inch leather strap, four inches wide with a wooden handle.[35] Particularly popular in the 1920s was the use of the "pole," a piece of wood beveled upward with rough edges that the inmate would be forced to straddle for hours without his feet touching the ground.[36] Against this background, the 1923 legislation assigning the responsibility for all executions to the Texas Prison System instead of the counties and mandating the use of the electric chair instead of hanging went virtually unnoticed.[37]

Investigations of the prison system were common; legislative committees examined the system in 1913, 1915, 1923, 1925, and 1928. Each reported the same problems of mismanagement and prisoner abuse that had been so common during the convict lease system.[38] The first real reform effort followed the visit of a group of legislators and Governor Daniel Moody to the prison in January 1930. The Governor declared the prison was "not fit for a dog," and initiated changes beginning with the appointment of Marshall Lee Simmons as general manager of the Texas Prison System.[39] Simmons had served as a member of the Prison Board and well knew the problems of the troubled system.

Simmons, who had a reputation as a charismatic leader, took on the task of reforming the system and manufacturing a positive public image. One of Simmons' creations, The Texas Prison Rodeo, actually did improve the public perception of the prison. The Rodeo became known as the "fastest and wildest rodeo in Texas." It included performances by celebrities and dangerous feats by prison cowboys. The rodeo drew immense crowds, earning as much as one-half million dollars a year, before it ended in 1984 because the arena was structurally unsafe.[40] Other public relations tools were a baseball team that played semi-professional teams from oil companies, choirs that performed outside the walls, and a radio show broadcast from the prison. Simmons' other initiatives included a massive cleanup of the prison and improved living quarters and food; more respectful treatment of inmates; improved but still limited educational opportunities; and the introduction of new industries, such as the Justin Book Company, the license plate factory, and improved agriculture production. The living quarters for correctional staff were enhanced, and a sick leave policy also implemented.[41] However, criticism of Simmons for the continued brutal treatment of prisoners, especially the use of the "bat," finally forced his departure in 1935.[42]

At the time of Simmons' departure, Texas and the United States were in the midst of the Great Depression, and Texans were much more concerned with their own daily welfare than the conditions of the state's prisoners. Due to economic pressures, the legislature wanted the prison to become more self-supporting by selling additional agricultural and prison industry products. However, the Congress of the United States had passed a law that prohibited the sale of prisoner-made goods to anyone other than state agencies.[43] Loss of this revenue source made the future of Texas' prisons extremely grim, especially given the lack of strong leadership by the legislature and prison administration. It was as if the 7,000 prisoners in Texas were forgotten souls.[44] As a result of the inaction, Texas prisons continued to be some of the worst in the United States.[45]

Negative assessments of Texas prisons plagued the state. The Texas State Council of Methodist Women persuaded the legislature in 1944 to retain Austin MacCormick, the nation's leading authority on prison reform, to investigate the system. MacCormick visited each prison and farm and provided a detailed report of his findings.[46] He documented three categories of serious failings: 1) Inhumane treatment of prisoners with bad living and working conditions, along with brutal discipline, leading to mutilations and excessive escape attempts, as well as inadequate medical and rehabilitation programs; 2) Inefficient administration and poorly qualified and trained personnel; and 3) Inefficient production because of antiquated farming methods and few industries.[47] The report drew the attention and ire of many influential

Narrative of Neglect: Texas Prisons for Men

individuals and groups, including Governor Beauford Jester, numerous legislators, and some prison board members, which resulted in a new prison board. The new board charged the new General Manager, O. B. Ellis from Shelby County, Tennessee, to reform Texas prisons and bring modern agricultural practices to the system.[48] With this move and the legislation that abolished corporal punishment in prisons, the state of Texas finally began to abandon the principle articulated in *Ruffin v. Commonwealth* (1871) that "[the prisoner] is for the time being the slave of the State."[49]

Benchmarks in Texas Prison Growth

Year	Prisoners	Year	Prisoners
1849	3	1855	75
1860	182	1866	264
1870	489	1878	1,738
1890	3,199	1900	4,109
1912	3,471	1939	7,000
1940	6,070	1945	3,270
1947	3,270	1950	6,424
1953	7,781	1962	11,890
1972	15,709	1978	22,439
1983	36,769	1988	39,664
1990	48,320	1994	91,875
1999	149,930	2006	152,889

Source: Paul M. Lucko, "Prison System," in *Handbook of Texas Online*. Texas State Historical Society. (http://www.tshaonline.org/handbook/online/articles/jjp03), accessed November 8, 2010; Texas Department of Criminal Justice, http://www.tdcj.state.tx.us/index.htm (accessed April 20, 2008).

After World War II, a new era in Texas prisons arrived, led by Ellis and sustained by his immediate successors. Ellis faced the daunting task of reforming a system deeply in debt, which had over 73,000 acres of farm land but purchased food each year, and which had lost the support of the public and the policymakers.[50] Ellis proposed what came to be known as the "Ellis Plan." The Plan included initiating rehabilitation programs, improving living conditions for prisoners, creating a more scientific prisoner classification system, improving working conditions for guards, starting a prison industry program, and modernizing farming techniques.[51]

Ellis met his goals. Prison infrastructure improved as inmate labor built new prison industries, such as fences and gun towers to improve unit security, and kitchens, laundries, and other support facilities to provide better nutrition, clean clothes for inmates, and more sanitary living conditions. The prison also constructed new cellblocks, in addition to dormitories, which provided a safer environment, and added televisions to the common areas. Ellis also fired many brutal and corrupt staff employees and at the same time, he tripled salaries for correctional staff; and benefits such as social security and retirement plans, became part of the compensation package. The prison also built housing for staff and provided benefits, such as barber and laundry services for the newly-mandated standardized uniforms.[52] Ellis also mended strained relationships with the legislature that had frayed when previous officials had not only denied the truth of the MacCormick's report but also had continued to be obstructionists.[53] The prison system changed its name to the Texas Department of Corrections, and Ellis also received the new title of Director. He did not simply delegate, but also led the prison system, based on the information he acquired from his many visits to the various prisons and farms of the system.[54]

Dr. George Beto became the Director and Chief of Chaplains following the sudden death of Ellis on the eve of a Board meeting in November 1961. Beto, a former Lutheran minister and university president, had served on the Illinois Parole and Pardon Board, as well as the Board of the Texas Department of Corrections. Like his predecessor, he believed in directly managing the prison and frequently arrived at prisons without warning to visit and observe; a predilection led to the nickname of "Walking George." During his visits, he often visited directly and informally with inmates as they went about their activities. However, his use of force to resolve a work stoppage early in his tenure left no question as to who was in control of the prison.[55]

One of Beto's greatest accomplishments was the creation of the

Narrative of Neglect: Texas Prisons for Men

Windham School District, the first prison-based school system in the nation. All inmates with only a sixth-grade reading level became students, and were offered the opportunity to obtain a General Equivalency Degree (GED) at state expense. Beto also contracted with colleges and universities to provide classes at the prison and was the moving force in the development of Sam Houston State University's criminology program with its emphasis on research in corrections.[56] His concern for prisoners spurred the creation of a diagnostic center, where incoming inmates underwent extensive medical, mental, educational, personality, and aptitude testing to help determine their occupational abilities and other needs.

Beto clearly understood that the reality of managing Texas' prisons required the balancing of conflicting interests—humane treatment of prisoners and economic benefit to the state—along with expertise in media relations and mastery of legislative relations. He increased the number of prison industries and convinced the legislature to require state agencies to purchase agricultural and industrial products from the prisons and to encourage local governments to do so as well. The new products and services included furniture, janitorial supplies, school desks, bus renovations, and public record data conversions. He also expanded agricultural operations and continued Ellis' pattern of modernization.[57] The ordered, clean, and economically Beto-directed prison system became a model for the rest of the world. However, despite his sterling reputation among politicians and penologists, critics decried Texas' prisons as a modern plantation system powered by prisoner slaves, as well as the continued use of the building tender system that allowed prisoners to supervise and discipline other prisoners. Furthermore, he was criticized for his harassment and punishment of inmates filing lawsuits against the system.[58] Understanding that the corrections world as he knew it was disappearing and adhering to his promise to his wife to serve only ten years, Beto retired in 1972 with the correct prediction that "[t]hings are going to get worse before they get any better."[59]

Beto's hand-chosen successor was W. J. Estelle. Estelle, a former warden at California work camps and in Montana, clearly understood his mandate was to maintain the status quo of a highly-effective prison as measured by its low costs, low incidence of reported violence, high rate of inmate employment, and general cleanliness of the prisons. However, the surface placidness abruptly ended on July 24, 1974, when three gun-wielding inmates seized the library, and the longest prison siege with hostages in national history began. Two of the seventeen hostages, women teachers for the Windham School District, were killed as they were used as body shields by the prisoners during their escape attempt eleven days later.[60] In addition, criticisms of Estelle's continued use of building tenders, along with complaints of malfeasance in terms of government contracts, were becoming louder. Pressures from the expanding prisoners' rights movement was about to change the Texas prison system forever, an issue destined to be decided in federal court.

World War II had changed the structure of American society. The scope of the conflict had allowed minorities and women to assume roles in society previously closed to them. The civil rights movement of the 1960s grew to also encompass the rights of women and captives in total institutions, such as penal and mental facilities, as part of the broader social movement.[61] Courts had traditionally taken a hands-off approach to prisoner claims, and had deferred to the expertise of the officials in management of the prisons. Federal courts especially were wary, given the nature of the federal system, to intervene in the operations of state prisons. In the landmark decision of *Cooper v. Pate* (1964),[62] the United States Supreme Court confirmed that prisoners could sue for protection of their constitutional rights under The Civil Rights Act of 1871, more commonly known as 42 U.S.C. § 1983, in federal court, and Texas prisoners and their jailhouse lawyers quickly acted.

The hostile environs of the Southern District Court of Texas that had jurisdiction over most of the prison system and the Fifth Circuit Court of Appeals meant that prisoners were generally unsuccessful. However, the case of *Cruz v. Beto*,[63] which challenged Beto's barring of attorney Frances Jalet-Cruz from the prison, heralded the end of the system's untouchable status. In June 1972, David Ruiz filed a handwritten lawsuit against the Texas prison system, asking for declaratory and injunctive relief for violations of prisoners' constitutional rights.[64] Although Ruiz actually filed the lawsuit while incarcerated at the Wynne Unit, the petition focused on conditions at Eastham Unit, known as the "end of the road for prisoners" and for "'the Eastham way' of doing things: one part head knocking, one part line toeing, and two parts hard laboring."[65] That Ruiz chose to challenge the conditions at Eastham was significant as it was one of two prison units located in the jurisdiction of the Eastern District of Texas, where Judge William Wayne Justice presided. Justice was known to be receptive to controversial and complex litigation. He had ordered Texas schools to desegregate,[66] forced the reorganization of the Texas Youth Council reform schools that confined juvenile offenders,[67] and required the local junior college to admit students with long hair.[68]

Concerned about the activity of the jailhouse lawyers, Beto moved the most active ones to the Wynne Unit, supervised by one of his trusted lieutenants, Warden C. L. McAdams. There, McAdams placed them in the same cellblock and assigned to a "hoe squad" where they chopped cotton. The move had unintended consequences. The jailhouse lawyers combined their talents and produced a series of civil rights complaints.[69]

Ruiz's lawsuit was consolidated in 1974 with seven others and styled *Ruiz v. Estelle* for purposes of trial. Together, the petitions encompassed nearly all of the Texas Department of Corrections operations, and the suit became the largest prisoner suit in history.[70] That same year, the United States was appointed as *amicus curiae* and later intervened as a plaintiff. In addition, the courts approved a motion that permitted the action to become a class action.[71]

At the time the trial convened, the stakes were high as one of every ten prisoners in the United States was in the Texas prison system.[72] The trial was moved from Tyler to Houston, located in the Southern District, because of "substantial logistical and security concerns generated by the prospect of transporting and housing hundreds of inmate witnesses, most of whom were confined in the Southern District." However, Justice remained the trial judge.[73] According to Justice, following the years of discovery by the parties, "consumed 161 trial days, [during which] 349 witnesses have testified, [and] approximately 1530 exhibits [were] accepted into evidence . . . May I express the hope that none of us are involved in [a trial] of this length again."[74] William Bennett Turner, the nation's leading prisoner rights attorney, represented the inmates. The state fought long and hard to overcome Turner's attacks. However, some state practices, such as the prison's use of force and prisoner building tenders became impossible to defend.[75]

Justice finally issued his lengthy ruling in 1980. The *Ruiz* findings declared that confinement in Texas prisons equated to "cruel and unusual punishment" that violated the Eighth Amendment of the U. S. Constitution in five categories: overcrowding, security and supervision, health care, discipline, access to courts, and other conditions of confinement, such as sanitation, fire and work safety, and hygiene.[76]

The ensuing remedial orders and negotiated agreements forced the state to abandon its former practices and initiate extensive reforms. One of the requirements was the removal of inmate building tenders, an order that had an immediate and dramatic effect on the prison system. The building tenders, or non-paid enforcers, had permitted the state to employ a minimal numbers of correctional officers, which saved thousands of dollars each year. However, the building tenders were difficult to supervise or control. They could not be disciplined or fired as could an employee, and many of these "inmate guards" became a law unto themselves.[77]

The loss of the building tenders created a new problem—a power void in the cellblocks. Cliques and then prison gangs that had plagued California, Arizona, and New Mexico exerted ever more control inside the prisons, and cellblocks became places where the strong continually preyed on the weak. The numerical replacement of building tenders with correctional officers also took the state years and billions of dollars to accomplish. The intermediate effect was a rash of assaults and murders unlike any that the prison system had experienced in the past.[78]

During the trial and the enforcement stages, the prison system continued its obfuscatory, intransigent, and obstructive ways. Officials intentionally misled the appointed Special Master Vincent Nathan, the governor, the attorney general, members of the Board of Corrections, Judge Justice, and the public about compliance. Following a July 1987 hearing, Justice issued a contempt order with fines of up to $800,000 a day. Although never enforced, the threat certainly achieved its goal; and the newly-elected governor, Bill Clements, announced to the legislature that Texas would begin immediate compliance. Through August 1988, as required in the Civil Rights Act of the losing party, the state paid the lawyers and firms who represented the plaintiffs $3.9 million, and another $4.9 million was spent to defray the costs of the master's office.[79]

The effect of the litigation was a restructuring of inmate society, revision of use-of-force policies, protection of access to courts, and creation of a modern prisoner health care plan. Estelle resigned in 1983, ending an era of change that began with Ellis in 1948, but the litigation continued.[80] "After decades of litigation and reform, reams of stipulations and decrees were reduced to a brief final judgment in 1992. Many issues were closed out, and others were the subject of only global mandates."[81] In June 2002, thirty years of litigation in the case now styled *Ruiz v. Johnson* were terminated, followed a few years later by the death of David Ruiz.[82]

The state of Texas began the lengthy process of implementing the massive changes ordered by the federal lawsuit, changes that would take decades and cost billions of dollars. The newly titled Texas Department of Criminal Justice faced the challenges of evolving public policy. Southern states, including Texas, had seen huge population growth with increased levels of crime; and politicians met the public's demands "to get tough" on crime by imposing longer and harsher sentences, especially in drug cases. The result was a remarkable transformation of the Texas prison system.[83] In the 1990s alone, prison population increased 204.1 percent, or by approximately 100,000 inmates, with a concomitant increase of 124 percent in the number of correctional officers. The state built seventy new prisons, and, in a departure from established policy, scattered them across the state rather than in close proximity to Huntsville.[84]

In another drastic reversal from the past, communities clamored for prisons, and politicians eager to be seen as tough on crime and as providing economic boosts to their constituents were more than happy to assist. Towns recognized that prisons were, in many ways, model corporate citizens. They consume few natural resources, are permanent, unlikely to close their doors or move, and the labor force is steadily employed. In 1990, the Texas Comptroller of Public Accounts estimated the addition of a large prison payroll (800 jobs or more) and its multiplier effect would generate $59 million, while smaller prisons (260 jobs) would produce a $20.4 million total spending effect.[85] By 2000, it was noted that the $91 million budget amounted to $3 million spread across the state each day with another $3 million per day in operating expenses.[86]

The prison system that had once been a minor state agency located in rural east Texas morphed into a huge government operation, albeit one without strong leadership as there was a revolving group of directors during this period.[87]

Table 3
Texas Prison Leadership

Years	Name	Title
1848 – 1850	Abner H. Cook	Superintendant
1850 – 1858	James Gillaspie	Superintendant
1858 – 1859	James H. Murray	Superintendant
1859 – 1866	Thomas Carothers	Superintendant
1866 – 1867	James Gillaspie	Superintendant
1867 – 1869	Thaddeus O. Bell	Superintendant
1869 – 1869	C. E. Morse	Superintendant
1869 – 1870	N. A. M. Dudley	Superintendant
1870 – 1877	A. J. Bennett	Superintendant
1878 – 1888	Thomas J. Goree	Superintendant
1894 – 1899	L. A. Whatley	Superintendant
1899 – 1902	J. S. Rice	Superintendant
1902 – 1907	Searcy Baker	Superintendant
1907 – 1911	Jacob A. Herring	Superintendant
1911 - 1927	The Texas Prison Commission	NA
1927 – 1928	H. Walker Sayle	Acting General Manager
1928 – 1929	W. H. Mead	General Manager
1929 – 1930	W. A. Paddock	Acting General Manager
1930 – 1935	M. Lee Simmons	General Manager
1935 – 1935	Dave R. Nelson	General Manager
1935 – 1941	O. J. S. Ellingson	General Manager
1941 – 1948	D. W. Stakes	General Manager
1948 – 1957	O. B. Ellis	General Manager
1957 – 1961	O. B. Ellis	Director
1961 – 1962	Jack F. Heard	Acting Director
1962 – 1972	George J. Beto	Director
1972 – 1983	W. J. Estelle	Director

Narrative of Neglect: Texas Prisons for Men

1983 – 1984	Dan V. McKaskle	Acting Director
1984 – 1985	Raymond V. Procunier	Director
1985 – 1987	O. L. McCotter	Director
1987 – 1989	James A. Lynaugh	Institutional Director
1989 – 1994	James A. Collins	Institutional Director
1994 – 1995	D. Wayne Scott	Institutional Director
1995 – 2001	Gary Johnson	Institutional Director
2001 - 2003	Janie Cockrell	Institutional Director
2003 - 2006	Doug Dretke	Correctional Institutions Division Director
2006 - 2009	Nathaniel Quarterman	Correctional Institutions Division Director
2009 - Present	Rick Thaler	Correctional Institutions Division Director

Source: Texas Prison Museum, "Texas Prison System Leadership" (Huntsville, TX: Texas Department of Criminal Justice File Document, 2008).

The nation's third largest criminal prison system today houses more than 172,000 prisoners in ninety-six facilities, employs more than 40,000 (28,500 security staff alone), and the costs more than $2.8 billion per year.[88] The expanded role of the agency includes the oversight of over 400,000 offenders in community supervision and 80,000 offenders on parole.[89]

The Texas prison system has undergone a dramatic metamorphosis over the years. For many years the state neglected its prison facilities and underfunded their staffs. Today's prison system little resembles the old as Texas has met the "evolving standards of decency" mandated by the Constitution and the courts.[90] The newer physical facilities are built in pods, using modern technology of cameras and electronic controls instead of the telephone-pole cellblock construction although dormitories remain a mainstay. There are hospital, diagnostic, and mental health units, as well as units with programs for the aggressively mentally-ill, for the intellectually impaired, and for both youthful and elderly offenders. The system also maintains separate units for inmates from low to high risk, administrative segregation, and, of course, death row. The living conditions are clean, and the food is edible and nutritious. Where brutality once reigned, discipline is administered primarily by hearings with minimal due process at least, and the penalty is often a loss of privileges or segregation in a clean, well-ventilated, lighted cell, where inmates receive the same meals as other prisoners. Use of force is strictly regulated and monitored. Texas has grudgingly accepted reform,[91] and continuation of the transformation is insured by multiple layers of scrutiny, internal and external. Texas' prison operations are no longer shrouded and hidden from the public.

In spite of such sweeping changes, some things remain constant—correctional policy is subject to the vicissitudes of politics and the public's engagement. The prison is authoritarian, and the goal is control. Work remains a primary part of prisoners' lives. Life is still harsh and discipline, strict.[92] Seeds of neglect have begun to creep back into the prison. *The Houston Chronicle* reported in 2008 that correctional officer salaries were so low that vacancies numbered over 4,000.[93] Prisons previously dedicated as therapeutic communities and drug treatment facilities have been converted to traditional prisons.[94] The prison has less staff dedicated to treatment and rehabilitation. One of the authors of this paper, a retired Texas prison warden, issued reduction-in-force papers to one-third of the teachers and all of the drug counselors at his unit as one of his last acts before his retirement. Further insight into the reappearance of neglect of Texas is revealed by examining the fiscal resources of a similar correctional system. Texas spent $2.8 billion in 2009 on the Department of Criminal Justice while California invested $9.8 billion for the same period on its Department of Corrections and Rehabilitation.[95] Texas has made remarkable changes over the years as its prisons have evolved, but the question is whether the cycle of neglect will once again become the dominant paradigm.

(Endnotes)

[1] O'Lone v. Shabazz, 482 U.S. 343, 354 (1987).

[2] Texas Department of Criminal Justice, *The Evolution of Modern Texas Corrections* (1996). VHS. 14 min.

[3] Daniel J. Elazar, *American Federalism*, 3rd ed. (New York: Harper and Row, 1984), 115-116.

[4] Daniel J. Elazar, *American Federalism.*, 116.

[5] Rupert Norval Richardson, Ernest Wallace, and Adrian N. Anderson, *Texas: The Lone Star State*, 3rd ed. (Englewood Cliffs, NJ: Prentice-Hall, 1970), 15, 39.

[6] R. Craig Copeland, "The Evolution of the Texas Department of Corrections" [master's thesis, Sam Houston State University, 1980], 5.

[7] R. Craig Copeland, "The Evolution of the Texas Department of Corrections," 6.

[8] Lee Simmons, *Assignment Huntsville: Memoirs of a Texas Prison Official* (Austin, TX: University of Texas Press, 1957), 48-49.

[9] Lee Simmons, *Assignment Huntsville: Memoirs of a Texas Prison Official*, 49.

[10] Paul M. Lucko, "Prison System," in *Handbook of Texas Online*. Texas State Historical Society. (http://www.tshaonline.org/handbook/online/articles/jjp03), accessed November 8, 2010.

[11] Paul M. Lucko, "Prison System."

[12] Paul M. Lucko, "Prison System."

[13] Donald R. Walker, "Texas State Penitentiary at Huntsville," in *Handbook of Texas Online*. Texas State Historical Society. (http://www.tshaonline.org/handbook/online/articles/jjp03), accessed November 9, 2010.

[14] Paul M.Lucko, "Prison System."

[15] Paul M. Lucko, "Prison System."

[16] Donald R. Walker, "Texas State Penitentiary."

[17] Paul M. Lucko, "Prison System."

[18] M. K. Wisehart, *Sam Houston: American Giant* (Washington: Robert B. Luce, Inc.. 1962), 650.

[19] Walker, "Texas State Penitentiary."

[20] Gary Brown, *Texas Gulag: The Chain Gang Years* (Plano, TX: Republic of Texas Press, 2002), 50.

[21] Holt v. Sarver, 309 F. Supp. 362, 381 (E.D. Ark.1970).

[22] Paul M. Lucko, "Prison System."

[23] Donald R. Walker, "Convict Lease System," in *Handbook of Texas Online*. Texas State Historical Society. (http://www.tshaonline.org/handbook/online/articles/jjp03), accessed November 9, 2010.

[24] Donald R. Walker, "Convict Lease System."

[25] John G. Johnson, "Captial Boycott," in *Handbook of Texas Online*. Texas State Historical Society. (http://www.tshaonline.org/handbook/online/articles/jjp03), accessed November 23, 2010.

[26] Donald R. Walker, "Texas State Penitentiary."

[27] Gary Brown, *Texas Gulag,* 156.

[28] Steve J. Martin and Sheldon Ekland-Olson, *Texas Prisons: The Walls Came Tumbling Down (*Austin, TX: Texas Monthly Press, 1987), 7; Lucko, "Prison Systems."

[29] Donald R. Walker, "Convict Lease."

[30] Texas Department of Criminal Justice, *Texas Department of Criminal Justice* (Paducah, KY: Turner Publishing Company, 2004), 13.

[31] Donald R. Walker, "Convict Lease."

[32] Rupert Richardson, et al., *Texas*, 221.

[33] Texas Department of Criminal Justice, *Texas Department of Criminal Justice*, 61, 105.

[34] J. Keith Price, "O. B. Ellis and the Golden Era of Texas Prisons," *Texas Corrections* (4th quarter 2006): 4.

[35] Steve J. Martin and Sheldon Ekland-Olson, *Texas Prisons*, 14.

[36] Gary Brown, *Texas Gulag*, 157.

[37] Texas Department of Criminal Justice, *Texas Department of*

Narrative of Neglect: Texas Prisons for Men

Criminal Justice, 26.

[38] David M. Horton and Ryan K. Turner, *Lone Star Justice: A Comprehensive Overview of the Texas Criminal Justice System* (Austin, TX: Eakin Press, 1999), 224.

[39] Steve J. Martin and Sheldon Ekland-Olson, *Texas Prisons*, 12; Price, "Ellis," 4.

[40] David M. Horton and Ryan K. Turner, *Lone Star Justice*, 225-226.

[41] Lee Simmons, *Assignment: Huntsville*, 66-69, 85-90, 103, 108-113; Lucko, "Prison System."

[42] J. Keith Price, "Ellis," 4.

[43] *Hawes-Cooper Act*, Act of Jan. 19, 1929, 45 Stat. 1084 (1929); *Ashurst-Summers Act*, Pub. L. 74-219, 49 Stat. 494 (1935); *Walsh-Healy Act*, Pub. L. 74-846, 49 Sta. 2036 (1936).

[44] Texas Department of Criminal Justice, *Texas Department of Criminal Justice*, 15.

[45] Texas Department of Criminal Justice, *Evolution*.

[46] Texas Department of Corrections, *Texas Department of Corrections: 30 Years of Progress* (Huntsville, TX: Texas Department of Corrections, 1977), 24.

[47] Texas Department of Criminal Justice, *Texas Department of Criminal Justice*, 35.

[48] Steve J. Martin and Sheldon Ekland-Olson, *Texas Prisons*, 20.

[49] *Ruffin v. Commonwealth*, 62 Va. 790, 794 (1871).

[50] J. Keith Price, "Ellis," 6.

[51] Steve J. Martin and Sheldon Ekland-Olson, *Texas Prisons*, 19.

[52] J. Keith Price, "Ellis," 8.

[53] Texas Department of Criminal Justice, *Texas Department of Criminal Justice*, 35.

[54] J. Keith Price, "Ellis," 6.

[55] David M. Horton and George R. Nielsen, *Walking George: The Life of George John Beto and the Rise of the Modern Texas Prison System* (Denton, TX: University of North Texas Press, 2005), 111-113.

[56] David M. Horton and George R. Nielsen, *Walking George: The Life of George John Beto and the Rise of the Modern Texas Prison System*, 155.

[57] David M. Horton and George R. Nielsen, *Walking George: The Life of George John Beto and the Rise of the Modern Texas Prison System*, 121.

[58] Michelle Childers, *The Ruiz v. Estelle Class Action Suit: A Retrospective Policy Analysis of Efforts to Improve Health Care in Texas Prison,* PhD diss. (University of Texas at Austin, 2005), 190; Ben M. Crouch and James W. Marquart, *An Appeal to Justice: Litigated Reform of Texas Prisons* (Austin, TX: University of Texas Press, 1989), 123.

[59] David M Horton and Lee K. Turner, *Lone Star Justice*, 152.

[60] James P. Sterba, "Official Defends Texas Siege Toll," *New York Times*, August 5, 1974.

[61] Dean J. Champion, *Corrections in the United States: A Contemporary Perspective,* 4th ed. (Upper Saddle, NJ: Pearson Prentice Hall, 2005), 399.

[62] Cooper v. Pate, 378 U.S. 546 (1964).

[63] Cruz v. Beto, Civil No. 71-H-1371 (S.D. Tex. filed March 18,1976).

[64] Carl Reynolds, "The Final Chapters of *Ruiz v. Estelle*," *Corrections Today,* 64 no. 3 (2002), 108.

[65] Aric Press, Daniel Pedersen, Daniel Shapiro, and Ann McDaniel, "Inside America's Toughest Prison," *Newsweek*, October 6, 1986, 48.

[66] Frank R. Kemerer, *William Wayne Justice* (Austin, TX: University of Texas Press, 1991), 117.

[67] Frank R. Kemerer, *William Wayne Justice*, 145.

[68] Frank R. Kemerer, *William Wayne Justice*, 90-91.

[69] David M. Horton and George R. Nielsen, *Walking George*, 150.

[70] *Ruiz v. Estelle,* 550 F.2d 238 (5th Cir. 1974); Carl Reynolds, "The Final Chapters," 108.

[71] *Ruiz v. Estelle*, 503 Supp. 1265 (S.D. Tex. 1980).

[72] Frank Kemerer, *Justice,* 356.

[73] *Ruiz v. Estelle*, 503 Supp. 1265, 1276 (S.D. Tex. 1980).

[74] Steve J. Martin and Sheldon Ekland-Olson, *Texas Prisons*, 168.

[75] Steve J. Martin and Sheldon Ekland-Olson, *Texas Prisons*, 168.

[76] *Ruiz v. Estelle*, 503 Supp. 1265 (S.D. Tex. 1980).

[77] James W. Marquart and Ben Crouch, "Judicial Reform," 198.

[78] James W. Marquart and Ben Crouch, "Judicial Reform,"142.

[79] Frank Kemerer, *Justice,* 391-396.

[80] Michelle Childers, *Ruiz v. Estelle*, 188.

[81] Carl Reynolds, "The Final Chapters of *Ruiz v. Estelle,"* 108.

[82] Michael King, "Criminal Intent: As Ruiz ends, Texas Prisons—and the AG—Still Aren't Rehabilitated," *Austin Chronicle,* June 21, 2002, http://www.austinchronicle.com/gyrobase/Issue/column?oid=95448 accessed November 29, 2010; Associated Press, "David Ruiz, 63, Convict Who Won Reform With Handwritten Lawsuit, Dies," *New York Times*, November 15, 2005.

[83] Michelle Childers, *Ruiz v. Estelle*, 239.

[84] Texas Department of Criminal Justice, *Closing of a Millennium--Reviewing the Past Decade* (Huntsville, TX: Texas Department of Criminal Justice, 2002), i.

[85] Texas Comptroller of Public Accounts, "Communities Vie for Prisons*" Fiscal Notes* (January 1990).

[86] Carl Reynolds, "Cell Block Boom: The Impact of Texas Prison Expansion," *Texas Business Review*, February 2000, www.utexas.edu/depts/bbr/tbr/Feb.00.Reynolds.html, accessed November 4, 2010.

[87] Paul M. Lucko, "Prison System."

[88] William J. Sabol, Heather C. West, and Matthew Cooper, *Prisoners in 2008*, (Washington: Bureau of Justice Statistics, 2009), 17-18; Texas Department of Criminal Justice, *Annual Review 2009* (Huntsville, TX: Texas Department of Criminal Justice, 2010), 6, 11-12, 23-24.

[89] Texas Department of Criminal Justice, *Annual Review 2009*, 28.

[90] *Trop v. Dulles*, 356 U.S. 86, 101 (1958).

[91] *Sandin v. Conner*, 515 U.S. 472, 485 (1995).

[92] Texas Department of Criminal Justice, *Evolution*.

[93] Lisa Sandberg, "State Prison Guard Shortage Critical" *Houston Chronicle,* April 19, 2008.

[94] Jeff Malcolm and J. Keith Price, "The Rise and Fall of Drug Treatment in Texas. *Texas Corrections* (4th quarter 2004): 9.

[95] Texas Department of Criminal Justice, *Annual Review 2009,* 12; California Legislative Analyst's Office, "California Department of Corrections and Rehabilitation," (Sacramento, CA: California Legislative Analyst's Office, 2.

"'We Just Come in to See the Show': Velma Patterson's Sensational 1936 Hunt County Murder Trial"

By John Hanners

Velma Patterson died on January 2, 1993, in a hospital in Sulphur Springs, Hopkins County, Texas. Ninety years old, she died as she had lived, an enigma to the end. And to the vexation of those who want to know more about her character and motives, she also took with her the truth, a slippery thing to begin with, behind the events that made her one of the most notorious individuals in Northeast Texas history.

Patterson was a rebel whose lifestyle defied Northeast Texas notions of marriage, family, and decorum. She lived life on the wild side, gathering around her men, money, and liquor—lots of liquor, nearly all of it illegal. Nicknamed "Voluptuous Velma" by the newspapers, she was, in the lingo of the day, both a "looker" and a "fast" woman, who married four husbands by the time she was thirty-four years old.[1]

What separated Patterson from the rest of her flamboyant Great Depression contemporaries was that she stood accused of that most heinous of crimes—filicide. She was indicted, arrested, and tried in 1936 for murdering her two daughters, eleven-year-old Billie Fae and twelve-year-old Dorthy Leon.

Her trial drew national attention, attracted spectators in record numbers to a Hunt County courtroom gallery, and exposed some uncomfortable truths about the accepted Northeast Texas social order. Accounts from Greenville and Commerce newspapers and court records in Hopkins, Delta, Lamar, and Hunt Counties provide the known facts.

She was born Velma Williams on April 1, 1902, in Hopkins County. Her folks, hard-scrabble cotton farmers, were from the Cumby/Brashears area. In his Audie Murphy biography, Don Graham explains to non-Southerners that in the world of cotton farming, lunch is called dinnertime, dinnertime is called supper, and there is no cocktail hour. It was obvious early on that Velma wanted the cocktail hour but not the cotton farm. She married twenty-eight-year-old William Wesley

John Hanners is a Professor in the Department of Mass Media, Communication, and Theatre at Texas A&M-Commerce. He is also the founding co-editor of the Texas Theatre Journal

McCasland in Sulphur Springs in October 1917, when she was only fifteen-years old.[2] Velma claimed she married McCasland, called Vester by friends and family, out of spite. She loved another boy that her father objected to, so when McCasland showed up she ran off and married him. The couple came back to Sulphur Springs to live. When Prohibition came in 1920, Vester began his checkered criminal career running bootleg whiskey.[3] The couple had three children: William, Jr., Billy Fae, and Dorthy Leon.

Velma divorced McCasland in 1928 while he was serving his second state prison term for bootlegging. The two maintained a friendly relationship until the 1936 murder trial when they turned on each other with a vengeance. After the divorce Velma moved to Commerce, Hunt County, and from 1929 until 1931, she claimed that she was married to a railroad brakeman and bootlegger named Raymond W. Kelly.[4] The children apparently caused friction in their marriage, an omen perhaps of future tragic events. "We got along famously," Velma said of her relationship with Kelly, "until difficulties arose because of the children . . . he made me a good husband."[5] A more plausible reason is that Kelly was caught "transporting a load of illicit whiskey from Oklahoma" and went to prison. Rumors floated that Velma had turned him in to clear the way for husband number three.[6]

After the short-lived marriage to Kelly, Velma learned the hairdressing trade and opened up a beauty shop under her first married name, McCasland. Permanents were $2.50 and up, and finger waves, a hairstyle favored by Velma until her death nearly sixty years later, were twenty-five cents.[7]

She married a third time in 1932 to William R. "Willie" Patterson, yet another bootlegger, and the criminal partner of her first husband, Vester McCasland. Twelve years older than Velma, Willie was a fun-loving, practical joker and a divorced father of four children. He is listed in the *1935 Commerce City Directory* as a trader, but the only thing he seems to have traded was whiskey for money. Patterson was arrested several times for illegal possession, and he, like his partner McCasland, was little more than a bad-luck petty criminal with big intentions.[8] Patterson and McCasland loaded up their cars with whiskey, according to police records, in amounts ranging from eighteen to thirty-two gallons and delivered throughout Hunt, Delta, and Hopkins County.[9] Bootleggers and moonshiners in the area came from all walks of life.

However, most were farmers, men who had easy access to remote locations and the machinery necessary for producing the potentially-lethal hooch. The two most lucrative sales periods were the Christmas season and summer church revivals, where liquor provided holiday relief during the worst of the Depression—and, in the latter case, relief from overzealous preachers. Authorities likely caught Patterson and McCasland so often because of an early example of police profiling. Primitive suspension systems on 1930s automobiles meant that a load of whiskey forced a vehicle down low to the ground, making it easy for police to spot bootleggers. The accepted pursuit procedure was to shoot out the car's tires.[10]

Patterson, like Velma's first husband, McCasland, went to State prison for running whiskey. It appears that in their absences Velma took up the slack. She acquired a "maid," more likely a prostitute, an attractive, fiery woman named Annie Cooper, and the two of them set up house at Harrington and Fourth Streets in Commerce. The well-mannered children attended school regularly despite their unusual home life with its all-night parties, bootleg liquor, and prostitution. Velma was frequently absent, attending late-night dances in Wolfe City, Paris, and at East Texas State Teacher's College, where she and her dates were fixtures at the President's Annual Christmas Ball. It must have been quite a sight to see Velma cavorting among middle-aged professors and their prim, disapproving wives. Velma was described by a contemporary in 1934 as being a "tall, medium-framed woman with dark hair and a very neat and attractive person." The children attended Central School, where they were universally well-liked and "always . . . well dressed" by their mother.[11]

During the late summer and fall of 1935, Velma lived through two traumatic events that started a tailspin from which she never recovered. First, her husband, Bill Patterson, died from injuries suffered during an impromptu wrestling match with his brother Fred. He endured agonizing pain for several days, finally expiring of peritonitis during an emergency operation at a Greenville hospital. He was forty-four-years old.[12] After her trial, Velma claimed that Patterson was the only man she ever loved.[13] She used his life insurance money, $1,300, to buy a new house by the railroad yards in northeast Commerce.[14]

Then, on November 24, Velma was seriously injured in an automobile accident. Driving her late-model automobile to Shiloh, a small Delta County town, she took a curve on a county road at too high a speed, skidded on the wet highway, and slammed into a stalled car that had run out of gas. A third vehicle rear-ended her car. A woman passenger, a friend of Velma's, unidentified, but probably Annie Cooper, was thrown into a field. Velma suffered head injuries so severe that she was taken to a hospital in Allen, some seventy miles away to the west.[15]

Meanwhile Vester McCasland, paroled after his second prison stint, was living with his father in Sulphur Springs. In December he moved in with Velma to help care of the children. Soon after, he and Annie Cooper became lovers.[16]

Things then got tragically worse. Just after New Year's 1936, a mysterious illness struck eleven-year old Billy Fae. A local doctor diagnosed it as "intestinal influenza," and she suffered from convulsions, high fever, delirium, sensitive joints, and an inability to urinate. She lingered four agonizing days, dying at last on January 7.[17] On January 13 a paid advertisement in the Commerce *Daily Journal* read "In memory of Billie Faye [sic] McCasland . . . quiet, noble, gentle, obedient, and ambitious child."[18]

Then Dorthy Leon, Velma's younger daughter fell ill. She suffered horrible pains for several days, displaying all of her old sister's symptoms, before dying on February 16. Dorthy was twelve years old. Within six weeks, Velma had lost both of her daughters. The girls were interred in a family plot at Pleasant Grove Cemetery, just outside Cumby in Hopkins County.

The coincidences of the girls' deaths were too much for Hunt County Sheriff D.M. Newton. A World War I veteran and former Cotton Belt Railroad engineer, Newton did not buy the "intestinal influenza" diagnosis. It did not help his suspicions that party girl Velma was a member of a criminal enterprise that he seemed incapable of eradicating or even slowing down—arrests for bootlegging actually went *up* in dry Hunt County *after* Prohibition was repealed. Hunt County Prosecutor Henry Pharr convened a grand jury to investigate the deaths. Sheriff Newton simultaneously asked the Commissioners Court for an order to exhume the girls' bodies. Velma gave her consent, and the bodies were dug up. Bits and pieces of internal organs were removed and placed in glass jars, which were then transported to Dallas to the private laboratory of the noted chemist Dr. Landon C. Moore.[19] Moore, born in England and the Chief Chemist for the City of Dallas, as well as the grandson of a former Ohio governor, had earned a PhD at Harvard, where he taught chemistry to Franklin Delano Roosevelt. For the past thirty years, he had busily carved out a career and persona in Texas. His social schedule and cheery exploits brought him much attention in the local newspapers, with descriptions of his elite get-togethers at his mansion on Ekard Street. He had also once owned a motion picture house and a prize-winning filly named "Colonial Girl." However, his penchant for amusements later came back to vex him during Velma's trial.[20] He was as "connected" as possible, claiming as a brother the man who discovered helium.

Moore developed his unique rapport with juries early in his career. He had testified in a 1902 murder trial of a Commerce man accused of killing his wife with strychnine. Before a spellbound jury and a packed gallery, Moore injected a frog with strychnine, and as the assemblage watched the hapless amphibian die, Moore carefully pointed out the effects of the poison on the nervous system. He then dissected the frog, showing the jury how he looked for traces of strychnine.[21]

Now, thirty years later, Moore was comfortably middle-aged and at the peak of a distinguished career. He reported to Hunt County officials that he had discovered a "large quantity of poison" in Billie Fae's and Dorthy Leon's "viscera." The children were murdered with arsenic "administered in either food, medicine, or drink." A grand jury indicted Velma on March 31, and Sheriff Newton arrested her on the charge of murdering Billy Fae. He also jailed Vester McCasland and Annie Cooper as material witnesses.[22]

The reaction was electric. Reporters from across the country flocked to Hunt County and breathlessly recorded the personal backgrounds and daily doings of all the principals. Deputy Sheriff V.L. Delaney told reporters that a search of Velma's cell had turned up "a bottle of poison, a razor blade, and several letters, in which she gave instructions for disposition in the event of her death and also instructions for the care of her fifteen-year-old son."[23] The poison turned out to be a bottle of Lysol to disinfect her cell—Velma was always excessively neat—the razor blade, in fact, a knife. The suicide notes were apparently genuine.[24]

Velma told reporters, from the *Commerce Farm Weekly*, that she was innocent:

> I'm not a Christian. I have done things that a lot of

good mothers wouldn't do, but I firmly believe that God won't let an innocent person suffer for something they did not do. . . I am doing every thing I possibly can to get cleared. It cost plenty to get the children exhumed. I had to put up my house, sell my rings, and my people are spending all they have.

She explained that she had tried her best to be a good mother. She spent money on violin lessons for Junior, expression lessons for Dorthy, and tap dancing lessons for Billie Fae. "That was my only purpose in life," she cried, "to bring those girls up to be something."[25]

Meanwhile, down the hall her fellow prisoner, Vester McCasland, would have none of it. He blamed Velma squarely for the deaths. "That woman is mean enough to do anything," he said. "She framed me on a liquor charge in order to get me sent to the 'pen,'" all in an effort to effect a divorce so that she could consort with Raymond Kelly.[26] Rumors swirled that she had already turned on Raymond as well.[27]

The prosecutors, three courtroom veterans, first indicted Velma for Billy Fae's death, then reversed themselves and charged her instead with murdering Dorthy Leon. After several delays and a postponement, the trial began in earnest on Monday, April 27, 1936. Velma arrived in a "gay tailored suit bought especially for the occasion." She topped it off with a large blue hat with a large buckle at the front. Her skirt, "split in accordance with the fashion, revealed her shapely legs."[28] The prosecution offered the jury—twelve men, all cotton farmers—a two-pronged theory for the murders.

First, Velma had a lover, a wealthy Lone Oak cattleman named Jimmie R. Wallace. In the bluntest terms, the girls stood in the way of her relationship with Wallace, and their elimination, as Annie Cooper would testify, would leave her free to marry him.

Second, Velma had two life insurance policies worth $551 on Dorthy with the American Life Insurance Company, a considerable sum during the Depression and equal to half a year's income for many cotton farmers. The insurance motive probably was the reason the prosecution dropped Billie Fae from the indictment and replaced her with Dorthy. In the end it did not really matter. In an extraordinary move, the trial judge, Charles Berry, a long-serving and experienced jurist, allowed in full testimony about Billy Fae's death.

We Just Came in to See the Show

The defense, composed of an expensive cracker-jack team led by local attorneys Charles C. McKinney and G.C. Harris, insisted that 1) the flu medicine given to both Billie Fae and Dorthy Leon was a bismuth compound fatally contaminated with arsenic at a local drug store or 2) McCasland and Annie Cooper conspired to murder the girls for reasons unknown or 3) natural arsenic found in the ground at the girls' gravesite contaminated their remains during the removal process. G.C. Harris proved a particularly effective advocate. An iconic Texas lawyer, he was a man whose "down home manner . . . made him the literal embodiment of [a] dominating courtroom presence."[29]

The parade of witnesses, from respectable physicians and pharmacists to Velma's friends from the world of prostitution and bootlegging, fascinated a gallery made up almost entirely of dirt-poor farm women who traveled through rain and mud and unseasonably hot weather to attend. It was standing room only in the small courtroom throughout the seven-day trial. Most of the women were elderly, revealing, a newspaper man said, "weather-tanned work-drawn faces and crude clothing [that] mark them as coming right off the farm. Many brought their lunches and stayed in the Hunt County courtroom from 7 a.m. until the 5:00 p.m. recess." One said, "It's seldom something like this happens around here and we just come in to see the show."

And what a show it was! Judge Berry admonished the audience that he would not stand for "foolishness," but during the trial he banged his gavel frequently, trying in vain to hush the crowd that insisted on discussing among themselves each witness's testimony. Berry banned one woman altogether for refusing to take her crying baby outside. [30]

Dozens of witnesses testified to things like Velma's purchase of a popular rodent poison called "Rough-on-Rats," even though McCasland testified that he actually bought the packets and whether or not rats were present in the Patterson home. Newspapers dutifully recorded Velma's stylish daily outfits and commented on her carefully arranged brunette hair. She was described in terms more befitting a movie star than a desperate woman on trial for her life.

Annie Cooper and Vester McCasland testified about incriminating statements Velma allegedly made concerning her lover Wallace, her remarks that she soon would have enough money to repair her wrecked car, and her apparent callousness towards the dying girls. The star witness was Annie who, dressed in a fetching green lace-topped dress

75

and displaying a single finger curl at her forehead, testified that she was a divorcee who worked as Velma's maid. A volatile witness—she had, after all, just spent six weeks in the county jail—her "eyes frequently flash[ed] . . . [as] she bent forward in her chair and pointed her finger" at defense attorneys.[31] Expert witnesses testified to the pros and cons of contaminated bismuth used as flu medicine and possible arsenic contamination at the gravesites during exhumation.

The most important witness, however, was the gray-haired, rotund Dr. Landon C. Moore, former cinema and race horse owner, distinguished Harvard graduate and Dallas City Chemist. For two solid hours he described, in long and often excruciating detail, his methods of examining little bits and pieces of stomach, liver and kidneys. His findings, he said, were irrefutable: the girls had been poisoned with several grains of arsenic each, mixed in with their bismuth-based flu medicine, and probably soup as well, and fed to them by their mother.[32]

The defense countered as best they could with expert testimony of their own. They, too, reportedly had the bodies exhumed and examined, but the results were never announced or presented at trial. Harris tried his best to shift the blame on the pharmacist who prepared the bismuth solution or the nefarious team of McCasland and Annie Cooper. Friends, relatives, and beauty shop operators testified about Velma's fierce devotion to her children. The "sarcastic and belligerent" Cooper was recalled to the stand for cross examination and, defiant to the last, denied any sinister involvement in the girls' deaths. She testified that she took care of the dying children and that Velma was in bed with Jimmie Wallace the night Dorthy fell ill. Much was made of the fact that McCasland did not attend Dorthy's funeral, and Cooper suggested his non-appearance was the result of illness, although others testified that he was just too drunk to go.[33]

On the last day of trial, a Saturday, May 2, 1936, Annie showed up in a "white dress, her hair carefully waved, her face smoothly powdered." She didn't flinch when in summation defense attorney C.C. McKinney called McCasland "Annie Cooper's Man."[34] Velma appeared bright and cheerful throughout the summations, kissing relatives and shaking hands with friends. A special visitor that last day was Captain Billy Arnold, a mostly deaf 100-year-old Greenville pioneer. Judge Berry let him sit at the court railing, commenting that "any man who has lived 100 years deserves some special consideration." The spectators, who had paid dearly for their own seats, applauded.[35]

Prosecutor Pharr, summoning his full rhetorical powers, demanded the death penalty for Velma. Special Counsel James Benton Morgan, on loan from the State to help with the prosecution, blamed Velma's alleged murders on old-fashioned lust for Lone Oak cattleman Jimmie Wallace. Quoting from the *Song of Solomon*, Morgan declared that "a woman in the arms of her passionate lover is a slave."[36] A month before in the indictment, H.O. Norwood, second chair to DA Pharr, was more philosophical: "I don't know what was in her mind. We have just got to struggle and guess."[37] The jury, led by foreman Fletcher B. Bland, retired at 4:55 p.m. The one thing everyone had anticipated never occurred. Velma Patterson, to the gallery's disappointment, never took the stand in her own defense.

The jury deliberated until 3 p.m. the next day, and at 3:15 marched into the courtroom with their verdict in hand. District Attorney Pharr was absent, out of town visiting relatives. The other attorneys had to scramble to get to the courthouse on short notice and on a Sunday.[38]

The jury's verdict?

Not Guilty.

The courtroom erupted. Velma "shouted with joy as the verdict was announced." She ran to the jury box and shook hands with each jury member and the judge. She "bubbled over with enthusiasm . . . smiling and speaking animatedly." Velma's mother, a "devout member of the Holiness faith turned the courtroom into a semblance of a camp meeting when she shouted for several minutes."[39] The trial was finally over.

One of the jury members, Bill Riddle, who farmed just north of Commerce, later told a newspaper reporter that the jury immediately rejected the testimony of lovers Vester McCasland and Annie Cooper, and that decision made the final verdict inevitable. Judge Riddle told the jury that if they believed McCasland's and Cooper's versions of events, they would have to convict Velma. If they did not, they would have to return a "not guilty" verdict. "So there was nothing to do," Riddle said, "but turn her loose because we couldn't believe those two." Landon Moore, however, came in for special derision. "He was just an old windjammer," Riddle snorted, adding:

> The jury didn't care about how many times he'd been across the ocean or how he was the grandson of one of

the few Democratic governors of Ohio. Why, he told himself how he ran a picture show at Cooper and about owning a race horse. I'd rather believe a home doctor anyway.

Pharr's closing argument "made us all tired," he said. "I didn't even listen to him because I had my mind made up after the first day."[40]

However, Velma's troubles were not over. Sheriff Newton, smarting over her acquittal, slapped Velma with seven liquor violations to keep her in jail until District Attorney Pharr could charge her with Billie Fae's murder. Her total bail for the two crimes was $8,800. Nine people came forward to post the amount, but Newton rejected them all. Velma's lawyers filed a mandamus petition and, three weeks after her trial, she was finally released.[41] Her acquittal resulted in the political ruin of the sheriff, his deputy, and most of the elected prosecution staff—they were fired or voted out in the next election.

Velma was scheduled to be tried for Billie Fae's murder in November 1936, but the prosecution's ace witness, Dr. Moore, fell ill; the new political regime dragged its feet, and a second trial never took place. Two years later, State's Special Counsel Morgan was quoted as saying, "[I]f a jury wouldn't stick a woman on what we gave them the last time, there is no use trying," Newly-elected Sheriff Frank Wolfe thought the case "might as well be pushed back into some pigeonhole and forgotten."[42]

Velma did her best to fade into obscurity. She left Commerce to live with her parents in Charleston, TX, Delta County. Then, a year and a half after her trial, on November 27, 1937, she married her fourth husband, Newton "Bud" Bates, a small, wiry former professional wrestler turned dairy farmer.[43] She married Bates in Paris, Texas, under the name "Marie," her middle name, perhaps to throw reporters off her trail. The couple settled down on a small Charleston farm, joined the East Delta Baptist Church across the road, and Velma spent the next fifty-six years living the very life she had worked so hard to escape: Velma Williams McCasland Kelly Patterson Bates—farmer's wife. The self-confessed non-Christian is buried in the East Delta Baptist Church graveyard.

Nevertheless, Hunt County did not give up. Long after the girls' deaths, the District Attorney announced in 1958 that he was indicting

Velma anew, this time for murdering Billie Fae. The indictment eventually was dismissed "because evidence was not available [Chemist Landon had died in 1942] and the offence [sic] occurred more than twenty-two years ago."[44]

The verdict never answered the numerous questions the trial raised, such as if she did not do it, who did and why? Such questions created a mystery, an almost legendary quality around Velma Patterson, all of it negative.[45] But for an intense week in 1936, she was right where she apparently wanted to be—center stage—fighting for her life, unapologetic, a defiant woman thumbing her nose at social conformity.

Meanwhile, the victims of this story generated their own tangled narrative. There are *four* headstones marking Billie Fae and Dorthy Leon's graves in Cumby's Pleasant Grove Cemetery. Two sit at the back next to their step-father Willie Patterson's marker, and two are in the Williams family plot at the front. Their names are spelled differently.[46] Even in death the girls could find no single resting place.

(Endnotes)

[1] Peter Levine, "What Happened to Justice?" *The Philadelphia Inquirer*, 7 August 1936.

[2] Hopkins County (TX) Marriage Records, Book MA, Vo. 15, p. 211.

[3] *Greenville* (TX) *Evening Banner*, May 4, 1936. *The Dallas Morning News*, March 22, 1936.

[4] *Dallas Morning News*, March 22, 1936.

[5] *Evening Banner*, May 4, 1936.

[6] *Inquirer*, August 7, 1936.

[7] Clipping, *The Daily Journal* (Commerce, TX), June 1, 1932, Velma Patterson Vertical File [Patterson File], Commerce (TX) Public Library *Messenger*, January 19, 1933.

[9] Criminal Docket 508, Hunt County, Texas.

[10] See Bill O'Neal, "Bootlegging in Northeast Texas," *ETHJ* 22 (Fall 1984): 13-20.

[11] Kathy Dunham, "Notes," typewritten, Patterson File.

[12] *Daily Journal*, August 20, 1935.

[13] *Evening Banner*, May 4, 1936.

[14] *Inquirer*, August 7, 1936.

[15] *Daily Journal*, November 25, 1935.

[16] *Morning News,* April 29, 1936.

[17] *Morning News,* April 29, 1936.

[18] *Morning News*, March 17, 1936.

[19] *Daily Journal*, January 13, 1936.

[20] *Morning News,* March 12, 1936.

[21] *Morning News,* March 12, 1936.

[22] *Messenger*, April 28, 1936.

[23] *Morning News*, March 21, 1936.

[24] *Morning News*, March 21, 1936.

[25] Clipping, *Commerce Farm Weekly*, March 27, 1936, Patterson File.

[26] *Daily Journal*, April 14, 1936.

[27] *Daily Journal*, April 14, 1936.

[28] *Inquirer*, August 7, 1936.

[29] Jim Conrad, "Lawyers Dominated in Earlier Days" in "Blackland Memories," *Greenville Herald Banner*, December 2, 2002.

[30] *Daily Journal*, April 30, 1936.

[31] *Evening* Banner, April 29, 1936.

[32] *Morning News*, April 29, 1936.

[33] *Evening Banner,* May 4, 1936.

[34] *Evening Banner,* May 4, 1936.

[35] *Evening Banner,* May 1, 1936.

[36] *Morning News*, May 3, 1936.

[37] Hunt County Criminal Record 38, p. 689.

[38] *Morning News*, May 3, 1936.

[39] *Evening Banner,* May 2, 1936; *Commerce Weekly Farm Journal,* May 8, 1936, Patterson File.

[40] *Farm Journal*, May 8, 1936, Patterson File.

[41] *Morning News,* May 16, 18, 19, 23, 1936.

[42] *Daily Journal*, November 9, 1938.

[43] Lamar County (TX) Marriage Records, Vol. 39, p. 412.

[44] *The Commerce* (TX) *Journal,* July 16, 1997, Patterson File.

[45] Dee Rinkes-Marshall, a former archival librarian at Texas A&M University-Commerce, conducted numerous interviews with area residents concerning the Patterson case and amassed a wealth of folklore about Velma Patterson.

[46] The various spellings of the girls' names on grave markers, newspapers, court records, and letters include Billy Faye, Billie Fay, Billy Fae, Billie Fae, Billy Fay and Dorothy Leon, Dorthy Leone, Dorthy Leon. I have used the spellings laid out in the official court indictments.

East Texas Historical Journal

Together They Won: Sam T. Rayburn and the Fourth Congressional District During World War II

BY WILLIAM MCWHORTER

Many historians consider Samuel T. Rayburn one of the United States' most influential congressmen and Speakers of the U.S. House of Representatives. Thus, more often than not, historical research tends to focus much more on his presence in Washington D.C. and his role in national issues, such as the Lend-Lease Act and the Rural Electric Administration, rather than his duties as a representative of his Congressional District. Rayburn's participation in national war legislation certainly benefitted the nation, but it also paid dividends within his home district and allowed the people of the Fourth Congressional District of Texas to have a tangible role in waging and winning World War II.

Rayburn responded to the concerns and demands of his constituency prior to, during, and after World War II, and such a response had definitive consequences and significance. Rayburn used his power and seniority in Congress to not only help the United States counter totalitarianism, but to also enhance the fortunes of Northeast Texas. This article is an example of how we can explore intimate facets of a significant national political figure by removing him from his high-profile position in Washington, D.C., and placing him within his congressional district, we can begin to explore Rayburn's connection to his constituency—thus gaining a deeper understanding of the insight, motivation, and inspiration of this accomplished political leader.

In a temporary exhibit on display at the Sam Rayburn House Museum State Historic Site in 2006, the Texas Historical Commission (THC) interpreted Sam Rayburn as a political leader during World War II and focused on Rayburn's accomplishments for the Fourth District via his dual role as a U.S. Congressman and Speaker of the House. The exhibit built upon the newly commissioned THC multi-year, multi-faceted, "Texas in World War II Initiative," a program to honor and

William McWhorter is the Military Sites and Oral History Program Coordinator at the Texas Historical Commission in Austin.

preserve the memories of Texans who served in the armed forces during World War II and the contributions they made to the war effort. This well-received temporary exhibit that interpreted Rayburn's wartime activities at the district—housed within the museum's visitor center—offered one way to keep the interpretation of Sam Rayburn fresh and exciting and allowed visitors to explore another facet of Rayburn's life.

Between 1939 and 1941, America slowly, but steadily, prepared itself for an impending war. Rayburn's actions as a local Congressman and later as Speaker were critically important in promoting pre-war preparedness and the evetual efficient management of the war effort on both the national and congressional district level. According to professor and author Anthony Champagne, who has written extensively on the Speakership and Rayburn, "Rayburn was a master at orchestrating his politics between Washington and Bonham."[1] Prior to World War II, Congressman Rayburn's Fourth District grew to include seven counties: Collin, Fannin, Grayson, Hunt, Rains, Rockwall and Kaufman. Speaker Rayburn was aware that to win World War II the federal government would need to spend vast sums of revenue. In response to direct constituency requests for aid, Rayburn wrote directly to Secretary of War Henry Stimson on numerous occasions to procure federal facilities and revenue within the Fourth District. Throughout the pre-war mobilization years and during the war, Rayburn secured, increased, and utilized as many federal military projects as possible for his constituents. Such facilities included airfields, hospitals, prisoner of war camps, and home front defense industries.

Speaker Rayburn's Fourth District constituents frequently solicited him to speak on their behalf, and his power and seniority allowed him to successfully fulfill their requests. A perusal of Rayburn's personal correspondence demonstrates the Speaker's genuine concern and work for his constituents. Multiple volumes of correspondence, from before and during the war, between Rayburn and his Fourth District constituency chronicle his efforts to secure badly needed federal spending for his district still suffering the effects of the Great Depression.[2]

Shortly before American involvement in World War II, Rayburn assisted his constituents in various pre-war military preparedness programs. In Grayson County, Rayburn helped push through the legislation needed to procure funding for the construction of the Denison Dam-Lake Texoma project on the Red River, an undertaking that marked the largest government project in Rayburn's district during his congressional career. Authorized by the Flood Control Act of 1938, the United States Army Corps of Engineers began construction in 1939 to curb the region's susceptibility to flooding, as well as to create a source for hydroelectric power, conservation, and recreation. During the spring of 1943, the project gained regional notoriety when German *Afrika Korps* prisoners of war were used to clear trees in one of the first area work programs for enemy prisoners of war.[3]

A farmer in his earlier years, Rayburn knew the importance of good roads in order to transport crops to market. He worked diligently before the war to designate Texas State Highway 24 as a "Defense Highway," which he succeeded in doing in November 1941. Two and a half years later, Rayburn successfully shepherded the passage of the Farm-to-Market Roads Program in the Federal-Aid Highway Act of 1944, which greatly aided not only his district but the nation.[4]

As opportunities to assist his district appeared before and during the war so, too, did many complaints from his constituents, many of whom believed federal governmental spending projects neglected their region. Rayburn's district was a rural district, and the larger financial and industrial districts of Texas in Houston and Dallas, along the oil fields further to the west, quite often received the largesse of federal aid. The farmers, ranchers, and families of enlisted men in the Fourth District were upset with federal regulations on the workweek, which they believed unjust and untenable given their livelihoods. Union workers under the War Labor Board received time and a half pay for work over the set 40-hour workweek, hours that almost every agricultural worker in Northeast Texas exceeded. In a letter to Rayburn, a woman from Royce City (Rockwall County) wrote, "[F]armers, ranchers and soldiers all worked well over 40 hours per week and saw no such federal legislation enacted to reflect their laborious contributions to the war effort."[5] Although the Congressman considered such concerns sincere (and he indicated so in a reply to the woman), many complaints that made their way to the Speaker's desk were not as legitimate. Authentic concerns and complaints were mixed with those of political opportunists and naysayers. Rayburn, in August 1943, for the first time publicly referred to those who complained, while American soldiers fought and died, as "Grumlins."[6] In an attempt to prevent the decline of American morale, he coined a phrase that caught on both in national conversation and in political cartoons.

For many in the Fourth District life improved during World War II; for some the war caused great strain. Constituents complained to Rayburn on various topics, ranging from mandatory rationing of gasoline and rubber to the enlistment age for young males. Congressman Rayburn's rural constituents depended upon both gasoline and tires for their livelihoods. In a 1942 letter to Rayburn, a Fourth District constituent wrote, "I do not like to bother you with matters of this kind, yet it is a very serious matter with me . . . Last year I traveled 26,000 miles, and all I can get from the Rationing Board at McKinney (Collin County) is a B-Card. This will give me 470 miles a month, which will not allow me to hold my job."[7] Many letters written to Congressman Rayburn's office responded quickly to constituent letters, and with equal speed followed up with the appropriate officials. In this case, Rayburn's office contacted the local county tire-rationing board in an attempt to help gain an exemption. Throughout the war, Rayburn attempted to balance the delicate level between what was good for the country and what his district demanded of him, a complex position that often meant he was unable to do both. However, in other instances he was able to bring economic opportunities to his district at a time of great national and personal tragedy.

Prior to and throughout the war Rayburn made sure that Hunt County housed a number of federal projects and facilities. For example, similar to many Texas towns, the people of Greenville welcomed servicemen into their homes and businesses. Commerce became a location for a Civilian Pilot Training Program when it opened at East Texas State Teachers College in May 1940.[8] As beneficial as the program was to the local Commerce economy, the principal project in the county and, for that fact, the Fourth District during the war, was the Majors Field facility near Greenville. Rayburn used his influence to convince the Civil Aeronautics Administration that the site would be a prime location for a new airport, so in 1939 the Greenville Chamber of Commerce took over the airport project. President Roosevelt, in preparation for the possibility of war, next directed federal funds in 1940 toward the financing of new municipal airport construction across the nation.

Less than one month after the Japanese attack at Pearl Harbor, Hawaii, construction began in January 1943 on what would become the newly minted U.S. Army Air Corps facilities near Greenville. Rayburn announced in April 1942 that the government would officially convert the civilian air facility into military service with housing for nearly four thousand personnel and services for more than three hundred training aircraft. The Moore Construction Company rapidly turned the former cotton fields and woodlands into a military city, complete with runways and approximately two hundred buildings.[9] The Basic Flight Training School opened on January 5, 1943, and utilized BT-13 trainer aircraft that arrived from another of Rayburn's contributions to his district, Perrin Field near Sherman. Majors Field had three auxiliary fields to help accommodate the overflow of trainer aircraft from the mother field in Greenville, which provided the cadets ample room to practice their landing and night flying. Between Majors Field and its three satellites, the military built a city roughly half the size of Greenville in less than a year.[10]

A contingent of the Women's Army Corps arrived in early 1943 and worked in the hospital and administrative offices of the 385th Sub Depot Air and Service Command. Women Army Service Pilots (WASP) arrived for service in 1944 at Majors Field, and during their time at Majors Field the female pilots retrieved planes from farmers' fields and served as liaisons and test pilots. The military also recruited local Hunt County women to work at the air school. The women received sixty days of training in welding, wood mill-work, and hydraulics, and then went to work replacing men who went to war. The restrictions of the then segregated military meant that the African American soldiers assigned to Majors Field primarily served in the transportation platoon.

The mission of Majors Field changed in late 1944 from basic flight training to fighter pilot training. P-47 Thunderbolt fighters replaced the airfield's compliment of BT-13 trainers. The change in training mission also brought a new unit of foreign Allied flyers to the field when the Republic of Mexico entered on the side of the Allies. The 201st Fighter Squadron of the Mexican Expeditionary Air Force, the *Aguilas Aztecas,* arrived for training at Majors Field on November 29, 1944.[11] In less than half a year they completed their basic training and left, eventually arriving for combat duty in the Philippines.

The destruction of the Nazi regime in May 1945 meant the beginning of the end for Majors Field as an active military training facility. The military first placed it on stand-by status until the U.S.

Together They Won

Army Air Forces determined its future role, and like many airfields across the Lone Star State (and across the nation) toward the end of the war the military deactivated it on July 15, 1945. That November Rayburn and U.S. Senator Tom Connally assisted the City of Greenville and Hunt County to gain authorization for the airfield's conversion to local civilian use, and after the war the site attracted a number of aircraft industries to the town for many years.[12] In historian Thomas E. Alexander's book, *The Stars Were Big and Bright: The United States Army Air Forces and Texas During World War II,* Volume I, Greenville resident Vincent Leibowitz stated, "It [Majors Field] provided the threshold from an agrarian economy to an industrial one." Alexander responded, "The army airfield that ultimately emerged from the initially modest project proved to be a critical turning point in the city's history, reshaping and improving it forever."[13]

During World War II, Rayburn's powerful political position helped the Grayson County economy improve with both the Denison Dam project and Camp Denison, a prisoner of war camp that housed German prisoners used at the Dam project. Perrin Field, a Basic Pilot School, also opened near there in the summer of 1941. Perrin Field hosted four auxiliary fields: Gibbons, Gaskin, Bilbo, and Burton. To free up more men for overseas combat theatres of operation, the U.S. Army assigned the training school a unit of the Women's Army Corps (WAC), the 77th College Training Detachment for the instruction of air crews, as well as a Link Trainer detachment (which utilized flight simulators). The airfield closed In July 1945 and officially deactivated the following year, but the military reactivated it in 1948 as Perrin Air Force Base.[14]

Rayburn also assisted the efforts of Collin County to house the fifteen hundred-bed U.S. Army Ashburn General Hospital in McKinney, which opened on May 1, 1943. Named for Col. Percy M. Ashburn, the hospital had its own contingent of prisoners of war, who worked on various maintenance projects at the hospital. The hospital eventually became a Veterans Administration Hospital in January 1945; in his signature style, Rayburn lobbied hospital bureaucrats to hire locally. In doing so, Rayburn showcased at Ashburn General Hospital— probably better than at any other World War II site in his congressional district—the three core desires of the congressman for his northeast Texas constituency: financial opportunity for his constituents in the present, financial opportunity for years to come, and medical assistance to veterans returning home. In addition to the hospital, Collin County hosted Camp Princeton prisoner of war camp (at the former site of a post-Great Depression Farm Security Administration migrant worker camp), which the City of Princeton tapped for labor to produce various public works, most notably onion and cotton harvesting and the enlargement of the city's park.[15]

Rayburn's efforts in Kaufman County, primarily within the county's largest city, Terrell, resulted in the establishment of Camp Kaufman Prisoner of War Camp. Located at a former Civilian Conservation Corps facility, Camp Kaufman was actually a branch camp of Camp Mexia. Like similar POW facilities on the East Texas home front, the camp greatly assisted labor shortages in the county brought on by increased military service and better paying employment opportunities in wartime industries inside and outside of Texas. The enemy soldiers harvested two thousand acres of cotton that would have otherwise been lost, a significant benefit to the local economy.[16] The military placed another branch prisoner of war camp in the county at Farmersville, where prisoners of war once again provided labor for various area farms on projects such as onion harvesting. Of special note, Terrell held the honor of hosting both a unique and nationally significant site, the No. 1 British Flying Training School, where American instructors trained British flying cadets throughout the war. The facility opened after Royal Air Force pilots transferred from Love Field in Dallas to Terrell in August 1941. Like their American counterparts, these flying cadets needed ample air space to learn how to fly, and Boykin, Tarver, Griffith, and the #4 auxiliary fields all supported the Terrell base. The flying school closed on September 1, 1945; today the No. 1 British Flying Training School Museum in Terrell commemorates the facility's efforts in support of America's ally, Great Britain, during World War II.[17]

The major military project in Fannin County was Jones Field, one of many contract flying schools across Texas that served the U.S. Army Air Forces during World War II. Located north of Bonham, the airfield was originally dedicated as the Bonham city airport in November 1929. The Secretary of War approved building a flying school at the airport in June 1945, and the City of Bonham leased the land and began construction that summer. The school opened on October 4, 1941, and the 302nd Flying Training Detachment assumed command, eventually training hundreds of cadets until the military deactivated the school on October 15, 1944. Similar to the other primary fields in Rayburn's district, four auxiliary fields supported training efforts at Jones Field.[18]

Fannin County, Rayburn's home, received a small branch prisoner of war camp. A Veterans' domiciliary opened there in 1950 and catered primarily to Fourth District veterans who were unable to care for themselves. Rayburn met the hospital's incoming personnel administrator upon his arrival in Texas and, true to pattern, informed him of the importance of hiring locally for all of the facility's three hundred-fifty positions.[19] In addition to the airfields and training schools, Rayburn assisted in necessary wartime funding to extend city infrastructure to all the installations throughout his district and, in turn, created more jobs for the Fourth District's economy.[20]

Congressman Rayburn's efforts were not limited to military installations; the war had presented an opportunity to modernize the Fourth District in many ways. Various war-related industries located in the district, chiefly road and highway improvements, as well as the Lone Star Steel Plant, which opened in September 1943 and represented a new industry for the predominantly rural and agricultural Fourth District. Such projects were discernible, tangible symbols of Rayburn's sway in Washington and noteworthy for the small rural district legislator.[21]

Rayburn continued to use his political clout as the war began to de-escalate to extend the life of armed forces facilities, and when possible, divert action occasionally on such projects, or at least, turn over ownership of military installations to county and city governments.[22] The successful conclusion of World War II made demobilization the central concern of America's leaders. Citizens of the Fourth District had become accustomed to the increased federal spending within the district, the state, and the nation. Their fears of an unstable economy grew. Constituents appealed to Rayburn for help in retaining, in some capacity, the airfields, hospitals, and other assets in the district.[23] During the last year of the war, the federal government, under the Surplus Property Act of 1944, had begun to liquidate surplus property, so Rayburn helped his Greenville constituents retain and gain title to the buildings from Majors Field for veterans' vocational schools as well as other structures in Fannin County at Jones Field. A notable example involved Rayburn's assistance in aiding the Bonham Independent School District's request to obtain buildings from nearby Camp Maxey.[24]

Lastly, Rayburn received and responded to various requests in late

1945 from his farming constituents about the extended use of German prisoners of war after hostilities with Japan ceased. Their following year's onion and cotton crops were ready for harvest, and since most of America's soldiers had yet to return from abroad, farmers requested that enemy prisoners of war be retained at least until the end of the 1946 harvest. To the farmers chagrin Rayburn did nothing to aid their requests, noting that peace treaties required prisoners of war to be returned to their home nations in a reasonable amount of time after the end of hostilities.[25]

Interpretation of history is never constant. Historians constantly re-evaluate established perspectives of seminal events, such as the Second World War. New information and evolving patterns of thought compete with established historiography, a process which often produces a complex and competing view of how a historic person or event's relationship should be interpreted. Our view and understanding of the past evolves with each new generation. Rayburn worked throughout the war to bring federal investment to the counties and towns of the Fourth District; at the same time he insisted, whenever prudent and possible, to hire locally. The resulting economic development meant that a chiefly poor, rural, agricultural populace had the opportunity to increase its standard of living during the war. Moreover, Congressman Rayburn's efforts gave the people of the Fourth District the opportunity to patriotically contribute toward America's eventual victory in World War II.

(Endnotes)

[1] Anthony Champagne, *Congressmen Sam Rayburn*, (New Brunswick: Rutgers University Press, 1984), x.

[2] H.G. Delaney, Interview with William McWhorter, October 12, 2005, Bonham, Texas.

[3] D.B. Hardeman and Donald C. Bacon, *Rayburn: A Biography*, (Austin: Texas Monthly Press, 1987), 204-205; Sherman *Democrat*, "Propose $5,000,000 for Denison Dam," May 10,1939, Sam Rayburn Newspaper Folders, Sam Rayburn Library Museum; Handbook of Texas Online, "Lake Texoma;" Handbook of Texas Online, "German Prisoners of War;" Dorothy Hudgeons, *Speak, Mr. Speaker*, The Sam Rayburn Library Museum Newsletter, "The Denison Dam." No. 19, July 1988; Anthony Champagne, *Sam Rayburn: A Bio-Biography,*(New York: Greenwood Press, 1988), 25.

Together They Won

[4] D.B. Hardeman and Donald C. Bacon, *Rayburn: A Biography*, 315.

[5] Letter from Royce City to Sam Rayburn, Box 3R302, Folder Rockwall County, Royce City, Center for American History, University of Texas at Austin.

[6] D.B. Hardeman and Donald C. Bacon, *Rayburn: A Biography*, 279.

[7] Sam Rayburn, Letter from P.C. Williams to Sam Rayburn, referencing gasoline rationing in McKinney, January 20, 1942, Box 3R303, Folder Gasoline Rationing File, 1943, Center for American History, University of Texas at Austin.

[8] D.B. Hardeman and Donald Bacon, *Rayburn: A Biography*, 300; Anthony Champagne, *Congressman Sam Rayburn*, 54-56; Truman Richardson, "Sam Rayburn Dedicates Bonham Air Field," *Speak, Mister Speaker,* The Sam Rayburn Library Museum Newsletter, No. 27, October 1997; Kaufman County Historical Commission, *Yesterdays' News*, January/February/March 2006, Vol. II No. 1.

[9] Thomas E. Alexander, *The Stars Were Big and Bright: The United States Army Air Forces and Texas During World War II*, Austin: Eakin Press, 2000), 88.

[10] W. A. Caplinger and Jim Conrad, *A History of Majors Air Field, Greenville, Texas*, (Hunt County Historical Commission), 1-7; Thomas E. Alexander, *The Stars Were Big and Bright*, 89.

[11] W. A. Caplinger and Jim Conrad, *A History of Majors Air Field, Greenville, Texas*, 15-17; Thomas E. Alexander, *The Stars Were Big and Bright*, 92.

[12] Anthony Champagne, *Congressman Sam Rayburn*, 54; W.A. Caplinger and Jim Conrad, *A History of Majors Air Field, Greenville, Texas*, 15-17.

[13] Thomas E. Alexander, *The Stars Were Big and Bright*, 97.

[14] Sam Rayburn Papers, Letter from Sherman Chamber of Commerce to Sam Rayburn, referencing the Economic value Perrin Field has been to Sherman and Grayson County, May 2, 1950. Box 3R337, Folder Perrin Field, Center for American History, University of Texas at Austin.

[15] Anthony Champagne, *Congressman Sam Rayburn* 55.

[16] Anthony Champagne, *Congressman Sam Rayburn* 113.

[17] Kaufman County Historical Commission, *Yesterdays' News*.

[18] Scott D. Murdock, *Jones Field, Texas*, http://www.airforcebase.net/aaf/jones.html, First accessed on December 12, 2005; Champagne, *Congressman Sam Rayburn* 54.

[19] Anthony Champagne, *Sam Rayburn: A Bio-Biography*, 35; Anthony Champagne, *Congressman Sam Rayburn*, 55.

[20] D.B. Hardeman and Donald C. Bacon, *Rayburn: A Biography*, 300; Anthony Champagne, *Congressman Sam Rayburn*, 54-56; Truman Richardson, "Sam Rayburn Dedicates Bonham Air Field;" Kaufman County Historical Commission, *Yesterdays' News*.

[21] Sam Rayburn, Letter from Sam Rayburn to Frank M. Thompson, Sherman Chamber of Commerce Referencing the City of Sherman's desire to acquire an alcohol manufacturing plant for the production of synthetic rubber, January 18, 1943. Sam Rayburn Papers. Box 3R298, Folder 1943: City of Sherman. Center for American History. University of Texas at Austin; Melvin Sisk. Letter to Sam Rayburn from Melvin Sisk, Sherman Chamber of Commerce referencing the city of Sherman's appreciation for the benefit that Perrin Army Air Field, now Perrin Air Force Base was to the community, May 2, 1950. Sam Rayburn Papers. Box 3R337, Folder Perrin Field. Center for American History. University of Texas at Austin.

[22] Sam Rayburn. *Speak, Mr. Speaker.* Bonham, Texas: Center for American History. 1978.

[23] Anthony Champagne, *Sam Rayburn: A Bio-Biography*, 25.

[24] Sam Rayburn, Letter referencing the sale of Jones Field buildings, Bonham, Sam Rayburn Papers. Box SRH 3R334, Folder City of Bonham Aviation School at Jones Field, Center for American History, University of Texas at Austin; Sam Rayburn, Letter Referencing the sale of Auxiliary Air Field near Caddo Mills, Texas, Sam Rayburn Papers. Box SRH 3R334, Folder City of Bonham Aviation School at Jones Field and Folder City of Bonham: School Buildings Located at Camp Maxey, Center for American History, University of Texas at Austin; Sam T. Rayburn. Letter to Dr. M.P. Crabb, April 23, 1947, Referencing War Assets Administration and remaining buildings at Majors Field, Greenville, TX, Sam Rayburn Papers, Center for American History, University of Texas at Austin.

[25] Harry L. Holiday. Letter from Harry L. Holiday, Regional Director of the War Assets Administration, referencing the War Assets

Together They Won

Administration's automotive sale in Texarkana, Texas in December 1946, Sam Rayburn Papers, Center for American History, University of Texas at Austin; Sam Rayburn Papers, Letter Referencing Mr. P.C. Miller of Farmersville, Texas request that POW labor remain to process onion crop, November 27, 1945, Box SRH 3R316, Folder Princeton Prisoner of War Camp, Center for American History, University of Texas at Austin.

Interpreting Mr. Sam at Home: Is it Enough, Or Why Can't It Be All About Mr Sam?

By Carlyn Copeland Hammons

For more than twenty years, one book has served as the staple publication for anyone thinking about establishing a museum: *Starting Right: A Basic Guide to Museum Planning* is used by organizations such as the American Association of Museums, the Texas Association of Museums, and the Texas Historical Commission. They all recommend it as one of the first resources for community groups to study before moving forward with any museum plans. In clear and candid language, the author succinctly details what a museum is, what responsibilities the new founders will face, and in what order the planning steps should be completed.

For almost eighteen years, *Starting Right* helped guide substantial numbers of museums to a solid beginning. An updated edition appeared in 2004 that addressed current museum trends and issues. While some of these updates—including the role of technology and new professional standards—were quite predictable, a new chapter posed some important questions and a word of caution: It counsels—think twice before you begin a project to open a house museum.[1]

Such advice and the questions it suggests are notable. How many house museums already exist within a few hours' drive of the proposed location? How many show and say the same thing every time you visit? Have you visited one more than once? How many of these house museums are open half-days, on weekends only, or just by appointment?

How many are suffering from deferred maintenance to the point that even the casual observer can see it? Can a new museum—and should it even want to—compete with them for money, visitors, staff, and volunteers?

The author's point is simple: "The last half-century has seen many wonderful building museums develop; it has also seen many decline into a kind of limbo from which they never really prosper nor fully die."[2] The challenges facing museums today are great. It is not realistic

Carlyn Hammons is a specialist in the Museum Services Program at the Texas Historical Commission in Austin.

Interpreting Mr. Sam at Home: Is it Enough?

to function in the same old way and expect success—or even to stay in business at all.

Concerned parties have considered the challenges, not only individuals and groups who have contemplated beginning a house museum, but museum professionals and historic preservationists, as well. They have asked the hard questions not only to those with plans for future house museums, but also to those *six* to *eight* thousand existing institutions across America. Professional organizational studies continue to show that house museums across the country struggle with sustainability, and many now face a critical situation because they are seemingly out of touch with the needs of changing communities and perennially underfunded.[3] Even the president of the National Trust for Historic Preservation finally asked, "Are there too many house museums?"[4]

It is beyond the scope and purpose of this short article to investigate fully the predicament facing the house museums of our country, but it is important that any discussion that concerns the operation and programs of a historic house museum be prefaced with at least some mention of the current professional climate. There are approximately 502 small history museums in Texas. One hundred and fifty of them reside in historic houses.[5] The need to stand out and offer something unique is paramount. The prospective visitor needs to have a reason to choose to stop at one house museum over any of a host of others. A good example to analyze and measure is a small museum, such as Bonham's Sam Rayburn House.

The easy and most obvious operational attraction, of course, is "Mr. Sam." No other house museum can claim distinction as the Rayburn family "Home Place"—it is one of a kind. Few politicians can claim a career as distinctive as the one Sam Rayburn enjoyed. He, also, was one of a kind. Sam Rayburn held elective office for 55 years, including 48 consecutive years in the U.S. House of Representatives, and 17 as Speaker of the House.[6] Today, many historians consider him as one of the greatest U.S. statesmen ever. When he was not in the House in Washington, Rayburn was at home in Bonham, Texas.

On the surface, these might sound like enough interesting facts to sustain strong interest in a house museum dedicated to Mr. Sam. Upon closer examination, one discovers that even a unique figure such as Rayburn in this one-of-a-kind setting cannot exempt the museum from the difficulties facing all historic house museums. Shared difficulties, such as financial health, good maintenance plans, and accurate preservation, are all present for house museums, but one of the most challenging—and the one we will focus on here—is interpretation and its increased importance to museum exhibits and material culture.

Interpretative methodology has changed significantly in recent years. Successful museums must constantly evaluate and improve interpretive techniques and programs in order to keep up with changing and evolving populations and audiences. Age, migration patterns, education, economics, and belief systems—not to mention changing cultural values—are all factors that change and shape the way people understand the past.[7] As audiences evolve, and as their expectations of historic resources change, so too must the ways in which museums interpret resources.

The challenge is compounded by the fact that it must all happen in a virtually unchanging exhibit environment. Most objects on display in a typical historic house museum rarely change or move. The Sam Rayburn House Museum looks nearly the same as it did when it first opened thirty years earlier. The house is designed to capture a moment in time—1961, the year of Mr. Sam's death— thus it will continue to look the same thirty, sixty, ninety years in the future. This is the very essence of historic house museums. It is also the reason so many fall into the trap of the standard, object-based interpretation, and why interpretive programs, such as tours, often remain unchanged for decades.[8]

There was a time that such a presentation was enough. After all, this is very recent history—Mr. Sam died less than fifty years ago, and the house opened as a museum just over a decade after his death. In its earliest years, and to some extent today, many of Rayburn's contemporaries were still around. These people knew, admired, and respected him. He represented their interests and they appreciated what he did for them; farm to market roads, rural electricity, and the jobs in war-time industries meant a lot for these people. In some respects, many were in awe of Rayburn. After all, he was the second most powerful man in the U.S. government, and he lived in their backyard.

Being in his house and seeing his things was enough for most visitors and allowed them to forge personal connections with him. *This is Mr. Sam's hat. I remember when he wore it in the town parade. Here is where he sat and visited with presidents, senators, etc. I remember*

Interpreting Mr. Sam at Home: Is it Enough?

when President Truman came to the house; I shook hands with him right here in this spot.[9] They brought their children and grandchildren to the house so they could share memories. Previously, facilitating that trip down memory lane—and the resulting sense of nostalgia—was enough.

Declining numbers of visitors persuaded professionals that new practices were in order. As the population ages the people who personally remember Rayburn are vanishing; and audiences must now be educated about who he was, what he did, and why it was so important. But even that's not enough. People want more. Museums are moving away from the "great man" interpretation of history. Retaining the interest of visitors through the exploits and artifacts of a famous or wealthy head of household is no longer enough to sustain a historical museum. Such a one-sided interpretation occurs at the expense of the site's other features, activities, purposes, and relationships, and jeopardizes not only the museum's own credibility, but also its broad public appeal.[10]

As our audience becomes more diverse, museums must strive to entertain and attract them. Rather than focusing on information specific to the site, museums are finding it necessary to expand their interpretations to include multi-layered content that represents themes beyond the site boundaries, ones that extend to larger historical contexts.[11] One way to achieve such a goal is to identify the multiplicities that exist in any household and incorporate various perspectives in the interpretation.[12]

In the case of the Sam Rayburn House Museum, this can be accomplished by including the perspectives of other people with connections to the Rayburn Home Place, which can include any of the various family members who occupied the house through the years, the household employees—including cooks, groundskeepers, and farm hands—as well as the perspectives of Rayburn's constituents.

Throughout its history the house meant something different to each person. For Mr. Sam, it was a quasi-respite from his work in Washington, a place to connect with the people of his district. For members of his immediate and extended family, it was a home, a place of residence. For others it was a place to work, and for still others it was a place of personal connection to politics, a place to seek assistance for a political need. Exploring different perspectives provides the opportunity to build multi-layered and thematic interpretation, which in turn places the Rayburn household in a larger historical context. The museum is thus able to interpret many different aspects of the cultural, political, and social history of early-to mid-20th century North Texas—including the role of politics in rural life, race relations, women's roles, agricultural trends, and daily domestic life.

Every tour of the house includes a stop in the kitchen. When visitors see the Crosley freezer and the Chambers gas range, they understand that Rayburn enjoyed modern conveniences. However, did he really spend much time in the kitchen? Are stories from his perspective really the best ones for the kitchen to tell? Perhaps better told are the stories of the household cook who is naturally more intimately connected to the kitchen.

Thus, the House interprets through the eyes of Bobbie Phillips, a local African American woman who served as the Rayburn family cook for many years. Such an approach provides the opportunity to look beyond the physical evidence of the technological advances of food preparation, which gives the visitor the opportunity, and the museum the chance, to explore larger social and political issues. What other occupational opportunities did minority women like Bobbie have at this time? How is this kitchen, with its modern appliances, different from one she probably had at home? How would she and her family have benefited from some of Rayburn's more significant political accomplishments, such as bringing electricity and farm-to-market roads to rural areas? How much did her menu selection depend on the agricultural activities at the farm? What was her relationship with the Rayburn women of the house? How must it have felt to work in the home of the second most powerful man in the U.S. government, and yet not be a welcomed participant in the political process because of her color?

Opportunities for expanded interpretation are numerous. If the facility highlights the role that the house and its other occupants played in politics, it then broadens the interest for visitors. Rayburn's relationship with his rural constituency resulted in his career longevity and success. For example, how did early and mid-20th century rural politics affect the role that the Rayburn family members played in the Speaker's numerous campaigns? What about the social and domestic roles of North Texas women during the first half of the 20th century? Several Rayburn women lived in the house at various points during their lives—some were married, others widowed, and some never married at all. Another key point of examination can be the steady stream of constituents that visited with Mr. Sam in the sitting room of his house and asked for his help on all sorts of matters? What were the issues that concerned them most? Any number of the tangible objects already on display in the house can act as a springboard for some of these intangible themes.

Audiences must be able to relate to Mr. Sam and see him as human. Certainly, any facility devoted to him must acknowledge Rayburn's successes and the events and characteristics that made him unique, but it must also "stop short of inculcating an incapacitating awe"[13] and reveal his failures, his fears, and his weaknesses in an effort to impart a full, well-textured narrative of the man's life. One brief example of how the museum has begun such a task is the inclusion in the interpretive tour of a discussion of Rayburn's very brief marriage and subsequent divorce[14]. Many of his constituents never even knew of the marriage at all, and social and political rules of the time dictated that it remain quiet.

There are, of course, many wonderful opportunities to reach out and make a meaningful experience for visitors. All good interpretation rests on a solid foundation of research that is a costly and time-consuming activity. A responsible museum must commit itself to detailed research.[15] People expect to learn something when they visit historic house museums, and museums must commit to accuracy and honesty lest they risk their credibility.

Museums—and especially historic house museums—are now under scrutiny and must constantly demonstrate that they are meaningful, relevant, and sustainable to an increasingly diverse and evolving audience. The Sam Rayburn House Museum works continuously to introduce new interpretation to the site's programs, using the site-specific resources to tell broader, more inclusive stories that place the house, its objects, and its occupants into larger historical contexts.[16] We should not be afraid to ask new questions about the old stories and old objects even though challenging established views can be risky. We have to look at the objects in the house and tease out new stories that can lead to newer, more integrated, more comprehensive interpretations.[17]

History is never constant. Our view and understanding of the past evolves with each new generation, and museums must keep up with change. Only time can tell what the Sam Rayburn House Museum will interpret in twenty to thirty years, but one thing is for certain—it can't be all about Mr. Sam. That just isn't enough.

(Endnotes)

[1] Gerald George, *Starting Right: A Basic Guide to Museum Planning*, (Walnut Creek, CA: Alta Mira Press, 2004), Chapter 5, 56-59, is titled "And if You are Planning a Historic House Museum?" The paragraph that follows is a condensed and paraphrased version of the author's questions posed in that chapter.

[2] Gerald George, *Starting Right*, 58.

[3] The most notable of these is the 1988 survey of historic sites commissioned by the NTHP and the 2002 conference "Rethinking the Historic House Museum for the 21st Century" cosponsored by the NTHP and AASLH. The findings are summarized in Gerald George, "Historic Property Museums: What Are They Preserving?" *Forum Journal* 3, no. 1 (Summer 1989); Gerald George, "Historic House Malaise: A Conference Considers What's Wrong," *Forum Journal* 16, no. 3 (Spring 2002); Richard Moe, "Are There Too Many House Museums?" *Forum Journal* 16, no. 3 (Spring 2002); and Carol Stapp and Kenneth Turino, "Does America Need Another House Museum?" *History News* 59, no. 3 (Summer 2004).

[4] Richard Moe, "Are There Too Many House Museums?"

[5] Figures based on 2001 survey conducted by the Museum Services Program, History Programs Division, Texas Historical Commission.

[6] Texas Historical Commission, "Life and Politics," www.thc.state.tx.us/samrayhouse/srhlife.html.

[7] Patrick H. Butler III, "Past, Present, and Future: The Place of the House Museum in the Community," in *Interpreting Historic House Museums*, ed. Jessica Foy Donnelly, (Walnut Creek, Calif.: AltaMira Press, 2002), 36.

[8] Jessica Foy Donnelly, *Interpreting Historic House Museums*, (Walnut Creek, Calif.: AltaMira Press, 2002), 1-5.

[9] These are not provided as exact quotes or attributed to any particular visitor; they simply represent the types of memories shared by visitors.

[10] Jessica Foy Donnelly, *Interpreting Historic House Museums*, 1.

[11] George McDaniel, "At Historic Houses and Buildings: Connecting Past, Present, and Future," in *Public History: Essays from the Field*, eds. James B. Gardner and Peter S. LaPaglia (Malabar, Fla.: Krieger Publishing Co., 1999), 244-45.

Interpreting Mr. Sam at Home: Is it Enough?

[12] George McDaniel, "At Historic Houses and Buildings: Connecting Past, Present, and Future," 245.

[13] Mike Wallace, "Visiting the Past: History Museums in the United States," in *Mickey Mouse History and Other Essays on American Public Memory* (Philadelphia: Temple University Press, 1996), 27.

[14] The tangible objects that lead to this revelation is the set of wedding china on display in the dining room, just one of many sets of china in the Rayburn home.

[15] George McDaniel, "At Historic Houses and Buildings: Connecting Past, Present, and Future," 241-44.

[16] The National Endowment for the Humanities awarded an Interpreting America's Historic Places Consultation Grant to the Sam Rayburn House Museum in early 2007. That grant allowed for research activities as well as a roundtable forum and workshop with a team of Rayburn scholars.

[17] Rex M. Ellis, "Interpreting the Whole House," in *Interpreting Historic House Museums*, (Walnut Creek, Calif.: AltaMira Press, 2002), 68.

East Texas Historical Journal

Book Notes

By Archie P. McDonald

The *East Texas Historical Journal* continues to provide reviews of recently published Texana elsewhere in each issue, plus this column of personal reactions of a curmudgeon and notes on various media of interest to East and other Texans.

A case in point is *The House Will Come To Order: How The Texas Speaker Became a Power in State and National Politics*, by Patrick L. Cox and Michael Phillips (University of Texas Press, Box 7819, Austin, TX 787813-7819, $40). Cox and Phillips narrate the development of the office through biographies of all the white males who have filled the post of Speaker of the Texas House of Representatives from Reconstruction through 2010—Ira Hobart Evans through Joe Straus— and at the same time trace the evolution of the nature and power of the office itself. Speakers served only one term during the nineteenth and early twentieth century, essentially taking a turn presiding over debates and expecting to return to the ranks during the next session. The office— and the man who held it—gained greater power when Coke Stevenson stretched his tenure to a second term, and later speakers (especially Billy Clayton, Gib Lewis, and Tom Craddick) who served even longer reached the pinnacle of power in Texas politics. Conventional wisdom held that the state constitution, in effect since 1876, so limited the governor's authority that the lieutenant governor actually wielded more power through the legislative process. Cox and Phillips believe that the Speaker of the House has surpassed both in determining the direction of state government. One way or another, I have met most of the speakers since Price Daniel the Elder and liked most of them. I judged Clayton most knowledgeable about the state's budget and affairs, Lewis the most fun to be around, but Craddick the most powerful and partisan. I recommend everyone interested in Texas government read this book; it is the best analysis of our public affairs to appear in some time. I strongly recommend page 181: this is the best explanation of why things are as they are that I have ever seen.

And from across the Capitol comes *How Things Really Work: Lessons from a Life in Politics*, by Bill Hobby with Saralee Tiede (Dolph Briscoe Center for American History, The University of Texas

Book Notes

at Austin, distributed by Texas A&M University Press, 4354 TAMU, College Station, TX 77843, $29.95). Bill Hobby served as Texas' lieutenant governor longer, and some would argue better, than any other individual and is unquestionably qualified to teach civics lessons, although Texans—voters and legislators—may continue to experience lapses in judgment. Hobby observes that we don't need any new laws because we already have criminals in sufficiency and that every dollar invested in education saves hundreds otherwise lost to ignorance and poor health. That is so obvious that one wonders why so many people do not understand it. Hobby's memoir includes introductory remarks by former Governor Dolph Briscoe, Don Carleton, and Tiede as well as a personal account of the public service of his parents, Governor William P. Hobby and Oveta Culp Hobby—first commander of the Women's Army Corps and a cabinet officer in the administration of President Dwight D. Eisenhower. In other words, public service is in Hobby's genes as well as his jeans. Herein he confesses mistakes—a rarity in political memoirs—and lets a surprisingly sharp partisan side show through. Those on that same "side" will chuckle while others choke. In a word, this book is "delightful."

Decision Points, by George W. Bush (The Crown Publishing Group, A Division of Random House, Inc., 1945 Broadway, New York, NY 10019, $35), is the inevitable memoir of the forty-third president of the United States. Other than "41," President George H. W. Bush, all recent presidents AND first ladies have provided an apologia—if not the "last word"—about their administrations. President George W. Bush, or "43," gives his take on such decisions as quitting drinking alcohol, running for governor of Texas, not to allow certain stem cell research, response to terrorists' attacks, going to war in Afghanistan and Iraq, response to Hurricane Katrina, and the late term military surge and financial crisis. Former President Bush is as partisan and political in print as he was in office, but here he was able to concede mistakes and shortcomings, something he famously declined while still in office. He is more personal and more human in this post-administration revelation than he ever permitted of himself while still in office. He is also loyal to those who served in his administration, finding little if any fault with their performances. President Bush admits *Decision Points* is just that and not a full memoir. He still generates a visceral response from friend and foe, but this is, at least, his side of these arguments.

And now for a memory: *Private Stock* from a celebrated Texas cooking school and restaurant...the Stockpot etc., by Claire Foster and Betty Hurst (P.O. Box 366, Longview, TX 75606 or info@privatestockcookbook.com). This one takes me back to my dark-hair days when Betty Davis of Longview showed up in my graduate classes. After a semester, Betty figured out a way to bring graduate instruction to Longview: she convinced our administration to offer classes there and fifteen friends enrolled in them. Also she always brought lemon squares to the class until her husband, Charley Davis, accused Betty of "cooking her way through school." The cooking helped, but then Betty was an All-A kind of girl anyway. Judy and I enjoyed Charley's and Betty's hospitality at their home and Cherokee Lake house on many occasions. There we met Claire and Henry Foster and Pat and Brew Houston, and learned of their many civic activities—including catering social events as fundraisers for various causes and their attendance at cooking schools in Europe. I don't know which husband suggested they get some tax advantage from such trips by starting a restaurant (but it sounds a lot like Charley Davis). Result: the Stockpot, named for an essential in a French kitchen, which provided the finest cuisine in East Texas for a while. Betty, Claire, and Pat brought some of the world's top chefs to Longview—Julia Childs and Wolfgang Puck head the list—to share their recipes and techniques with the ladies' friends. Even old history professors got to go to the Stockpot on occasion. Pat is gone now, but Betty and Claire keep Longview a lively place. And, yes, the recipe for lemon bars is included, in case you want a master's degree—and can write a publishable thesis! Lerner and Loew said it best, "Don't let it be forgot, that once there was a spot . . . called . . . the Stockpot."

The best-illustrated book to come our way in quite some time is *Gymnosperms of The United States & Canada* (Bruce Lyndon Cunningham Productions, 180 County Road 8201, Nacogdoches, TX 75964, $75), by Elray S. Nixon with illustrations by Bruce Lyndon Cunningham. Nixon was a former colleague in SFA's Department of Biology and the region's foremost botanist, now retired to Utah, and Cunningham is Nacogdoches' resident nature artist. Nixon tells the reader/viewer what a gymnosperm is (our pines are in that group), and all about plant identification, names, appropriate terminology, and distribution; Cunningham supplies nearly 200 pages of absolutely breathtaking colored drawings that show how the pine tree looks from

Book Notes

its needles to cones to a cross section of trunk. I can but fall back on Al Loman's claim that "folks who like this sort of thing will like this sort of thing" because I know most East Texas historians would not know a gymnosperm by that term if they ran into one. But we know pines, and some other trees, too, and nowhere will one find them illustrated any better.

Similarly, but without the color illustrations, is Fred Tarpley's *Wood Eternal: The Story of Osage Orange, Bois D'Arc, Etc.*, (Tarpley Books, 4540 FM 1568, Campbell, TX 75422, $13). Fred, who previously taught us about Texas place names, East Texas words and sayings, and Jefferson, Texas—especially in his *Jefferson: East Texas Metropolis*, part of the Ann and Lee Lawrence Series—brings now his considerable research and narrative skills to teaching us about the infernal and wonderful hardwood that has blessed and bedeviled generations of East Texans. History and folklore are blended here with Fred's usual skill and success.

While we are growing things, let's look at Cheryl Hazeltine's *Central Texas Gardener*, with photographs by Cheryl and Richard Hazeltine, No. 45 in the Louise Lindsey Merrick Natural History Series (Texas A&M University Press, 4354 TAMU, College Station, TX 77843, $24.95). So Central Texas isn't exactly EAST Texas, but we claim some of it anyway. As defined by Hazeltine, Central Texas claims Tarrant and Dallas counties on the north, Bexar County on the south, Brown and Gillespie counties on the west, and Leon and Madison counties on the east. Hey, we have a few members in Dallas, anyway. Much of Hazeltine's advice works anywhere, such as selecting the correct plants for sun or shade, soil type, or other variables. Information extends to gardening tools, design, lawns, trees and shrubs, vines, flowers, and vegetables, and a concluding chapter ominously titled "Trouble in the Garden," which turned out to be about pests, not Original Sin. Wonderful color photographs of plants for all seasons.

An Extraordinary Year of Ordinary Days (University of Texas Press, P.O. Box 7819, Austin, TX 78713-7819, $24.95) is Susan Wittig Albert's journal for 2008, her sixty-ninth on the planet but a year of revelation (the energy crisis), celebration (Barrack Obama's political victory), and contemplation (alternating living in the Texas Hill Country and the Sangre de Cristo Mountains of eastern New Mexico). The author says her lifestyle is enabled by writing—so far—seventeen

China Bayles mysteries, juvenile books, and books about women and literature. In addition, she writes a daily journal entry on the events of Her Day—from the ordinary to the extraordinary, and claims no felicity of style for them. On the contrary, most are well written, and reveal an active and inquiring mind. This is an extraordinary book.

The Lincoln Assassination: Crime and Punishment, Myth and Memory, edited by Harold Holzer, Craig L. Symonds, and Frank J. Williams (Fordham University Press, 2546 Belmont Ave, University Box L, Bronx, NY 10458, $27.95), contains essays by Holzer, Williams, Richard Sloan, Thomas P. Lowry, Elizabeth D. Leonard, Thomas R. Turner, Edward Steers, Jr., Michael W. Kauffman, and Richard Nelson. Current exploring of the old, old story of the death of the nation's sixteenth president—the first to die in office by gunfire. This collection brings together the thoughts of some of the nation's leading students of Lincolniana, especially Williams, the scholar/chief justice of Rhode Island's Supreme Court, who has been the leader in this field for more than two decades and served as the ETHA's Max S. Lale Lecturer in September 2001. See especially his chapter titled "The Lincoln Assassination in Law and Lore."

Hers, His & Theirs: Community Property Law in Spain & Early Texas, by Jean A. Stuntz, with foreword by Caroline Castillo Crimm and preface by Gordon Morris Bakken (Texas Tech University Press, Box 41037, Lubbock, TX 79409-1037, $35) tells how things came to be in Texas—from who could kill whom and for what to why what's mama's is mama's and what's yours is mama's, too. At least, that is the way some folks tell it, but Caroline Crimm and Jean Stuntz will set you straight on the roots and branches of Texas' legal system and community property. My cutesy deference to chauvinism aside, this is a serious study of a serious subject, done well.

The Moodys Of Galveston & Their Mansion, by Henry Wiencek, with foreword by Robert L. Moody, Sr. and epilogue by E. Douglas McLeod (Texas A&M University Press, 4354 TAMU, College Station, TX 77843, $19.95), is Number Thirteen in the Press's Sara and John Lindsey Series in Arts and Humanities and is, as expected and appropriately, celebratory. "Moody" and "Galveston" are synonymous. I have been visiting the city for more than six decades, and no visit leaves undone a drive past Ashton Villa or the Moody Mansion on the boulevard. I was even offered the opportunity to stay there when

Book Notes

presenting a program in Galveston, but declined; what if I had damaged it in some way, even by accident? I did get a personal tour from then curator Pat Butler, and have been back since, too, and always marvel at the period opulence of the place. Good coverage of the Moody family, too, especially Mary Moody Northen. My favorite photo in the book appears on page 69—Northen with John Wayne. The Duke is dressed in fedora, dark suit, and white necktie and holds a handkerchief in his hand. Must have been a humid day on The Island.

Finally, the good folks at Plano's Convention and Visitors Bureau sent along a copy of Robert Lawson's *Ben and Me: An Astonishing Life of Benjamin Franklin by His Good Mouse Amos* (Little, Brown & Co, New York and Boston, 1939, reissued 2010, $6.99), a juvenile biography which loosely follows Franklin's life but attributes his successes to the advice of Amos, a mouse who lived in Franklin's fur cap. It reminds one of Jeff Guinn's *Autobiography of Santa Claus*. Clever, and like Franklin, the "autobiography" does dispense good advice for an orderly life. If you go to Plano, tell the CVB folks thank you.

Book Reviews

On the Prairie of Palo Alto: Historical Archaeology of the U.S-Mexican War Battlefield, by Charles M. Haecker and Jeffrey G. Mauck (Texas A&M University Press, 4354 TAMU, College Station, TX 77843-4354), 1997. Contents. Illustrations. Preface. Notes. Glossary. Bibliography and Selected Annotations. Index. P. 227. $29.95. Softcover.

The Battle of Palo Alto was the first major battle of the Mexican-American War. In this battle, Zachary Taylor's Army of Occupation fought General Mariano Arista's Army of the North on disputed ground approximately five miles north of present-day Brownsville, Texas. Here, twenty-four hundred American troops collided with thirty-four hundred Mexican troops as a response to the Mexican besiegement of Fort Texas. The end of this battle decidedly proved the Mexican army an inferior opponent to American forces. Mexican soldiers were under-trained, used the outdated military techniques of Napoleon, and had cumbersome artillery that kept them from moving quickly against America's more modern "Flying Artillery." Traditionally, historians conveyed these events through political and military history. Recent years, however, have seen an increase of cultural histories on the Mexican-American War, including *On the Prairie of Palo Alto: Historical Archaeology of the U.S-Mexican War Battlefield*. Even though it adheres to the traditional Mexican-American War narrative, this book takes a non-traditional approach by incorporating archaeological discoveries with cultural history to explore the topics of American victory and Mexican deficiencies.

On the Prairie of Palo Alto: Historical Archaeology of the U.S-Mexican War Battlefield, co-authored by historical archaeologist Charles M. Haecker and historian Jeffrey G. Mauck, provides an interdisciplinary approach to analyzing the events and outcome of the Battle of Palo Alto, the first battle of the Mexican-American War. Using evidence from a 1994 archaeological dig at Palo Alto and battle maps as primary sources, Haecker and Mauck determine the history and consequences of the battle.

Haecker and Mauck divide the text into six chapters. The first chapter serves as an introduction to the topic as it provides the historical context of the Battle of Palo Alto, the purpose of the book, and the research used to write the book. The next four chapters include a historical overview of the battle; a discussion of the weapons, accoutrements, and the soldiers; a topographic and documentary analysis; and a survey of the physical evidence of the battle. The sixth chapter, a conclusion, restates the goals of this book and explains how those goals were accomplished. It also examines the historiography of the field, discusses the importance of this work, and considers how it can contribute to future research.

The biggest asset of this book is the incredible use of photography and maps. These photographs allow the authors to maintain their story line while keeping readers focused and engaged with the subject. Without the photographs, many of the discussions on artillery would become dry, possibly alienating many non-military readers. In addition to these amazing photographs, there are images of battle maps created by Mexican-American War officers. These maps, which can be found throughout the book, help the reader understand battlefield tactics as well as the location of events in relation to the entire battle. This enables the reader to form an idea of place and imagine the battlefield as something other than grass and debris. For example, the fifth chapter of the book is dedicated to "The Physical Evidence of the Battle" (133-155); and here the authors explore many weapons, ammunition, and uniforms used by both American and Mexican soldiers. In conjunction with the text, the authors supply grids and high-resolution photographs to make the material more understandable and engaging.

The Mexican-American War has typically been viewed as the finale to the Texas Revolution and the precursor to the Civil War. It is frequently overlooked and underappreciated, and the histories written about it usually only summarize a few battles. Hopefully, with the publication of cultural histories, such as *On the Prairie of Palo Alto: Historical Archaeology of the U.S-Mexican War Battlefield*, memory of the Mexican-American War will be more dynamic and nuanced.

Pamela Ringle
Tomball, TX

Myth, Memory and Massacre: The Pease River Capture of Cynthia Ann Parker, by Paul H. Carlson and Tom Crum (Texas Tech University Press, Box 41037, Lubbock, TX 79409 -1037), 2010. Contents. Illustrations. Appendix. Notes. Bibliography. Index. P. 195. $29.95. Hardcover.

"There is a great deal of history in myth and folklore which is good," state the authors of *Myth, Memory and Massacre*. "But sometimes there is too much folklore and myth in history" (87).

Authors Paul H. Carlson (retired professor of history at Texas Tech University and a resourceful and innovative researcher/author/speaker) and Tom Crum (retired district judge and current president of the East Texas Historical Association) have examined a legendary historical incident and have proved it to be rife with folklore and myth—and fabrications. The incident under the Carlson/Crum microscope is the "Battle" of Pease River. On December 19, 1860, L.S. "Sul" Ross, a young Texas Ranger captain and future governor, led an attack against a small Comanche hunting camp on the Pease River in northwest Texas. There were about forty Anglo attackers, including a score of U.S. cavalrymen. Seven Comanches were killed, including four women, and three were captured while a handful managed to escape. Two of the captives were thirty-four-year-old Cynthia Ann Parker and her baby daughter.

Cynthia Ann was nine years old in 1836 when a large Comanche war party attacked the stockaded settlement of the Parker clan. Several settlers were slain, and Cynthia Ann and her little brother were among the captives. Her brother was recovered, but Cynthia Ann grew up as a Comanche. She became one of the wives of Peta Nocona and had three children. Her oldest son, Quanah, was destined to become a noted warrior and chief. Cynthia Ann's recapture a quarter of a century after the Parker Massacre distinguished the Pease River action from numerous similar clashes during the period.

Paul Carlson and Tom Crum have traced the distortion of this incident from an attack on a small, defenseless encampment to a battle against as many as 600 Comanches, including 150 to 200 warriors. "Chief" Peta Nocona (who was not a chief and was not present at the Pease River) purportedly was killed after fierce combat. There were numerous other embellishments, most of which were created to promote the ascendant career of Sul Ross. Still in his twenties, Ross

Book Reviews

rose from private to brigadier general in the Confederate Army. In 1873 Ross was elected sheriff of McLennan County, and in 1880 he won election to the state senate. Having discovered the political benefits of publicizing his heroics in Civil War combat and in the 1860 battle which rescued Cynthia Ann Parker, Ross encouraged friends and supporters to emphasize his military exploits in military literature. The Pease River fight became wildly exaggerated, helping Ross to an overwhelming victory in the 1886 governor's race. Following two productive terms as governor, the combat hero became president of the Agricultural and Mechanical College of Texas, serving until his death in 1897.

The authors carefully re-examined and compared the accounts of the Pease River fight, particularly those of participants. They found diary alterations, missing reports, and outright falsehoods in first-hand testimony, all contributing to the exaggeration of a minor raid into a mythic battle. Because of this fabrication for political gain, a fictional version of the Battle of Pease River has been accepted for generations. The authors located original, true accounts of the modest action of 1860 while skillfully tracing the evolution of the myths and fabrications. In addition to presenting an accurate version of the Pease River raid, Carlson and Crum performed an impressive work of historiography – "a clear example of how memory, in this case collective memory, is manufactured more than recalled." (130) Historians should utilize these methods to reexamine other mythic, long-accepted incidents of 19th century Texas.

Bill O'Neal
Panola College

Los Brazos de Dios: A Plantation Society in the Texas Borderlands 1821-1865, by Sean M. Kelley (LSU Press, 3990 West Lakeshore Dr., Baton Rouge, LA 70808), 2010. Contents. Acknowledgements. Introduction. Prologue. Abbreviations. Appendix. Appendix 2. Notes. Bibliography. Index. P. 283. $42.50. Hardcover.

Los Brazos de Dios: A Plantation Society in the Texas Borderlands 1821-1865 is a remarkable study which expands our understanding of one of the most prolific plantation regions of Antebellum Texas. It also affirms the value of local and regional historical studies as a tool underscoring similarities and differences of frontier borderland plantation societies compared to other plantation areas in the Antebellum agricultural South.

Sean M. Kelley's volume spans the 1820s arrival of the earliest Anglo settlers in the Lower Brazos River Valley—the counties of Brazoria, Fort Bend, Austin, Washington, and Grimes—to the close of the Civil War. Many of these settlers, particularly the well-to-do, brought with them slaves, evidently hoping to recreate the plantation agricultural society they left behind in more established southern states to the east.

In some respects, the culture they created strongly resembled what they left behind. It also significantly differed as a result of the demographic diversity unique to the Lower Brazos. In addition to the Anglo majority and their slaves, the region had significant minorities of German immigrants and African-born slaves.

The former comprised about thirty percent of the region's free population. Although a few German settlers eventually purchased slaves, the majority in German communities looked askance at the peculiar institution. Even though most Germans were reserved in their criticism of slavery during the decade preceding the war, Anglos increasingly perceived their immigrant neighbors as a subversive element that was dangerous to the established order. The diversity of the Lower Brazos was further enhanced by a small but evident number—Kelley guesstimates 500 by 1837—of African-born slaves transported via the Middle Passage to Cuba and ultimately smuggled into Texas to work on cotton and sugar plantations.

Further complicating the nature of this rich, varied, multicultural frontier milieu, the Lower Brazos was a borderland plantation society. Consequently, Kelley's work becomes an unprecedented examination of slavery as a borderland phenomenon. The region's geographic proximity to Mexico conditioned the outlook of the river valley's slave population. If official antebellum Mexican policy on slavery in Texas remained ambiguous, Mexico's unqualified rejection of slavery south of the border was a temptation to slaves with dreams of freedom. More than a few such Lower Brazos refugees found redemption south of the Rio Grande. These factors combined to make slavery in this particular local context less stable than in America's older plantation regions. Kelley even-handedly explores relationships within and between each of the area's four population groups in terms of class, gender, and master and slave.

The book's uniqueness lies not only in the exploration of how a borderland plantation society differs from plantation regions securely ensconced to the east, but also in Kelley's informed judgments concerning the character, origins, and significance of the Lower Brazos African-born slaves. Although the author refreshingly acknowledges his lack of traditional resources, Kelly boldly makes persuasive, intuitive leaps based on credible circumstantial arguments combined with shards of archaeological evidence, slave narrative excerpts, and the 1870 population census. The author reconstructs the story of Anglos, Creole slaves, and Germans through the use of more conventional evidence, including plantation ledger books and collections of planter papers, census and courthouse records (particularly succession documents, inventories, divorce records, and court proceedings), election returns, county tax records, and contemporary newspapers and periodicals of the day.

With these tools, Kelley creates a fascinating sociological tapestry reconstructing Lower Brazos society in all its complexity. His deft selection of detailed anecdotal accounts provides concrete illustrations of the evolving character of marriage, family structure, gender relations, and the master-slave interaction. Kelley not only recounts the stories of representative individual planter families but also, perhaps more importantly, gives occasional voice to their more anonymous plain folk neighbors and bondsmen. He has initiated a discussion certain to yield new understanding of the plantation economy's diversity and breadth.

From beginning to end, Kelley provides a delightful, informative read. His highly descriptive, compelling style, combined with exquisitely interesting introductions, pull the reader effortlessly forward. From the "Introduction," which places his examination in its larger historiographical context through the "Epilogue," which summarizes his persuasive, articulate arguments and explains why the war and emancipation mark a distinctive chronological divide, Kelly makes an important, ground-breaking contribution to the literature on American slavery and plantation society.

Rick Sherrod
Stephenville, Texas

Nassau Plantation: The Evolution of a Texas German Slave Plantation, by James C. Kearney (University of North Texas Press, 1155 Union Circle #311336, Denton, TX 76203), 2010. Contents. List of Illustrations. Acknowledgements. Introduction. Appendices. Notes. Selected Bibliography. Index. P. 353. $32.95. Hardcover.

James C. Kearney has written an original and insightful work on an often-overlooked aspect of the Society for the Protection of German Emigrants in Texas (*Adelsverein*)—he Nassau Plantation, an attempt to set up a slave plantation by German noblemen in the 1840s near present-day Round Top. Drawing heavily on the reports, letters, and documents contained in the Solms-Braunfels Archives, Kearney traces the development of the plantation from the formation of the *Adelsverein* in Germany to its beginnings in Texas, the rise of the plantation as a valuable asset to the Society, and finally to the eventual demise of the plantation. The result is a wealth of new information on German-Texan history.

Kearney's first chapter on the formation of the *Adelsverein* and its conception as a society to promote German emigration to Texas is outstanding. The society believed the best approach was investment in a slave plantation modeled on an almost feudalistic system, in which the plantation replaced the castle. In an effort to accomplish this, the Society sent Joseph Count of Boos-Waldeck to Texas in 1842. Despite the Count's misgivings about a large-scale immigration project, he preoccupied himself with the task of establishing Nassau Plantation, the centerpiece of his program and vision. Boos-Waldeck purchased seventeen slaves in New Orleans and Houston and began work on the plantation in March 1843, the pre-eminent building of which would be a "dog trot" called the *Herrenhaus*. The Count completely underestimated the difficulties of setting up a plantation on the Texas frontier and returned to Germany in December 1843, leaving German Texan Charles Fordtran in temporary charge of the plantation. Three slaves soon ran away, two of which were never recovered.

Prince Solms-Braunfels arrived to replace Boos-Waldeck in July 1844. Upon arriving at Nassau, the colorful and pompous prince was disgusted with the *Adelsverein*'s association with slavery, remarking that slavery "is a true stain on human society, and something completely unworthy of our Society." Despite his condemnation, the plantation served Prince Solms well as a convenient and comfortable home base from which to conduct the business of the Society, specifically preparing for the first boatloads of settlers who began arriving in the winter of 1844-1845. The Prince stayed at the plantation on three separate occasions before returning to Germany in June 1845. That same year, in response to criticism in Germany, the *Adelsverein* declared its new colonies "slave free zones." Ironically, the German settlements the Society later established became hotbeds of anti-slavery and anti-secessionist sentiment.

John O. Meusebach succeeded Solms-Braunfels as commissioner-general, and he too spent time at Nassau during the first months of 1846 before he attempted to move colonists onto the Fischer-Miller grant. At this point the plantation was essentially leaderless, and in an improbable twist a slave rose to become overseer of Nassau Plantation for a good part of the year 1847. By fall of the same year, it became painfully clear to the leadership in Germany that plans in Texas had not worked but instead taken a disastrous turn when a shootout at the *Herrenhaus* left two dead. The shootout at the plantation set into motion a series of events that culminated in the dismemberment of the plantation. The revolution of 1848 in Germany created further turmoil.

Into the leadership void at the plantation stepped Otto von Roeder, who by the Civil War became the largest German-Texan slaveholder in the state. As a gristmill owner, he organized shipments and supplied grain to desperate colonists in New Braunfels and Friedrichsburg in 1846, 1847, and part of 1848. By the summer of 1848, the Society's debt to Otto von Roeder rose to $6000. In 1850, von Roeder gained control of the Nassau Plantation in exchange for the assistance he had provided. He began to parcel off the plantation and sell it to fresh immigrants from Germany, transforming the region into one of the most exclusively Germanic areas of the state.

Kearney deftly illuminates the importance of the Nassau Plantation. It had historical significance as the first and most important possession of the *Adelsverein* from beginning to end. The plantation served above all as a reservoir of value that could be parlayed into food and other desperately needed supplies. Although it failed miserably as an experiment in slavery, the plantation's supportive role gave newcomers from Germany a chance to get established in Texas. *Nassau Plantation* is a welcomed addition to German-Texan history and should remain the definitive work on the subject for decades to come.

Matthew D. Tippens
Abilene, Texas

Texas Confederate, Reconstruction Governor: James Webb Throckmorton, by Kenneth Wayne Howell (Texas A&M University Press, 4354 TAMU, College Station, TX 77843-4354), 2008. Contents. List of Illustrations. Series Editor's Forward. Introduction. Notes. Bibliography. Index. P. 251. $29.95. Hardcover.

Foregoing the grandiose scope (and necessary limitations) of a traditional biography for a more practical, focused, and nuanced examination, Kenneth Wayne Howell reviews the central decades in James Webb Throckmorton's life, paying closest attention to the defining aspects of Texas politics that in various ways shaped the career of a man remembered for both his political pragmatism and principled defiance, both preceding and following the American Civil War. Like most good political biographies, Howell largely succeeds in contextualizing the life of his subject within the broader scope of the subject's times. In this case, scholars interested in knowing more about the psychology of antebellum or Reconstruction-era Texas or about Texas political culture more generally will find much utility in this volume. In several small ways, Howell shows Throckmorton to be a reflection of a multiplicity of ideological and philosophical impulses, ranging from his Whiggish protectionism of small farmers against the more dominant and emerging planter class to his distrust of federal interventionism; his antipathy of political extremism; and, ironically, his defense of white supremacy. Along those lines, Howell also discusses with reasonable clarity and insight Throckmorton's evolving position on issues of race, particularly in the post-slavery era. Like the state he eventually and briefly came to lead, Throckmorton's views on race were repugnant but also relatively superficial. He actively resisted and denied equality for the freedman, though also like many Texans, he arrived at those positions for reasons that transcend simple bigotry and even reflect strands of early populism.

Almost by default, Howell's study will certainly stand as the definitive biography of Throckmorton for some time to come. Still, the fact that Howell fills an obvious void in both the historiography

Book Reviews

of nineteenth-century Texas and political biography in no way detracts from what is a very readable, insightful, and engaging study of one of the Lone Star State's most intriguing and dichotomous leaders.

Sean P. Cunningham
Texas Tech University

The Chosen Folks: Jews on the Frontiers of Texas, by Bryan Edward Stone (University of Texas Press, P.O. Box 7819, Austin, TX 78713), 2010. Contents. Prologue. Acknowledgements. Introduction. Conclusion. Notes. Bibliography. Index. P. 294. $50.00. Hardcover.

The Jewish Diaspora is perhaps one of the greatest ethnic migrations in history and led to the settlement of Jews in nearly every part of the world, including Texas. However, as with most ethnic migrations in the late nineteenth century, settlement patterns tended to be concentrated in urban areas, owing to chain migration patterns as well as to the presence of established enclaves in the larger cities. The Texas immigration experience, on the other hand, poses a different story in that there were no established communities when larger numbers of Jewish settlers arrived. Texas was, in a sense, truly a frontier for ethnic migration. In *The Chosen Folks: Jews on the Frontiers of Texas*, Bryan Edward Stone explores how the presence of this frontier impacted Jewish settlement in the Lone Star State and how the immigrants sought to sustain and maintain their culture in such an environment—which often meant adaptations and compromises to the traditional Jewish way of life.

Stone argues that although there were earnest attempts to create Jewish settlement schemes in Texas—not unlike the German *Adelsverein*—most Jews did not consider the area as a first choice, instead preferring densely populated east coast cities, such as Boston and New York, as prime locations for settlement. The main reason, he maintains, is that Texas was a "frontier" region and offered few amenities for Jewish life—clerical access; availability of Kosher foods; and, above all, camaraderie—that the urban centers offered. A few adventurous early Jewish settlers, such as Nicholas Adolphus Sterne, to whom the author refers as "proto-Jews," exercised and observed few, if any, Judaic customs, traditions, or cultural practices.

After the Civil War, as immigration to the United States from

117

Eastern and Southern Europe increased, enthusiastic promoters attempted to convince Jewish settlers to forgo the urban centers and settle in Texas—which they promoted as a new "Zion." This "Galveston Movement" succeeded in bringing a sufficient number of Jews into the area, creating a fledgling ethnic community. By the early 20th century, the Jewish communities in Galveston, Houston, and Dallas grew to sufficient sizes that Judaic religious services and rites became accessible in most parts of the state.

The Jewish communities in Texas were quite vibrant as evidenced by the maintenance of several periodicals and benevolent organizations, as well as their share of internal politics. In the book Stone explores several issues pertinent to Jews at the time: the decision to support the international Zionist movement (the creation of a Jewish state), the choice to embrace "Reform" or "Orthodox" Judaism, and the debates on further settlement into the state. In the end, Stone maintains that the Jewish communities—despite their internal divisions—united in the face of issues such as the rise of nativism, the Second Ku Klux Klan, Nazism, and support of the Civil Rights Movement after World War II.

Throughout the book, Stone addresses the issue of the frontier within the Jewish-Texan communities. Here, he points out several compromises that Jews made while they embraced their "Texanness": using former gubernatorial candidate "Kinky" Friedman as an (perhaps extreme) example of this effort to sustain both Jewish and Texan identities. In researching the work, Stone relied heavily on dependable sources, such as oral accounts and personal correspondences, as well as the bourgeoning ethnic Jewish American press. The result is an excellent, groundbreaking account of an understudied ethnic group in Texas. *The Chosen Folks* addresses a need for more contribution to ethnic studies in Texas historiography.

Son Mai
McNeese State University

Book Reviews

Cowboy's Lament: A Life on the Open Range, by Frank Maynard; edited and introduced by Jim Hoy, with foreword by David Stanley (Texas Tech University Press, Box 41037, Lubbock, TX 79409-2010), 2010. Contents. Illustrations. Foreword. Preface. Acknowledgments. Glossary of Names. Bibliography. Index. P. 216. $29.95. Hardcover.

Jim Hoy and David Stanley have produced an excellent book which tells of the life and range adventures of Frank Maynard as a freighter, buffalo hunter, Indian trader and cowboy. Maynard started these adventures at age sixteen, and although he came back home from time to time, the free life on the open range kept drawing him back to the frontier.

The book is divided into four sections, plus the foreword and preface. A reader should not fail to read the foreword and preface, which contain much interesting reading and information. The introduction is a brief history of Frank Maynard's life and is followed by the second section that contains Maynard's own recollections of his adventures from 1870 to 1880. These adventures took him from Nebraska to Kansas and on herding trips through Indian Territory into north central Texas.

Maynard was a poet, and the third section of the book is devoted to several of his poems. Although Maynard referred to it as a song, included among these poems is one titled "The Dying Cowboy." The authors, as others have done, claim that with this poem or song Maynard was the first to take an old song, "The Bad Girl's Lament," and change the words to reflect the untimely death of a young cowboy or ranger. Although Maynard called his song "The Dying Cowboy," he referred to the dying young man as a ranger, meaning a cattle herder or range rider or simply ranger. Although much of the song remains the same as Maynard's original work, further alterations by other writers meant the song eventually became known as "The Cowboy's Lament" or "The Streets of Laredo," thus the book's title.

The book is more than a history of this song and Maynard's other writings. The preface is a good description of how serendipity often plays an important part in historical research, and anyone who has done such research can identify with the author's good fortune.

The introduction describes the life of Maynard from his birth in 1853 in Iowa City, Iowa, through his adventures, starting at age sixteen working first as a freighter and then as an Indian trader, buffalo hunter, and cowboy. It ends with Maynard's life in Colorado Springs, Colorado, where, after the settling influence of marriage, he became a carpenter and wrote several newspaper articles, which he titled "Maynard's Western Tales." These articles make up the fourth section of the book.

The authors include a glossary of names, which is helpful in identifying the many people Maynard tells about in his recollections and newspaper articles. Everyone who has an interest in the life of the working cowboy at the end of the open range will find this book an excellent addition to his or her library.

Tom Crum
Granbury, Texas

The Great Southwest Railroad Strike and Free Labor by Theresa A. Case (Texas A&M University Press 4354 TAMU College Station, TX 77843) Contents. Acknowledgements. Notes. Bibliography. Index. P. 279. $40.00

This is an impressively informed, judiciously argued, well-written monograph on the Great Southwest Railroad Strike of 1886. Readers of this journal will find much Texas history here with workers' communities from Marshall to Mineola to Palestine and Fort Worth playing leading roles in the dramatic events of the 1880s.

This work is an admirable blending of labor, social, political, and cultural history. While manifestly a "labor history" book, Case succeeds in making it much more. The densely-packed pages with details of engineers, firemen, brakemen, switchmen, shopmen, and track crews are not only necessary for understanding worker ideas of equality versus hierarchy on the job, but also provides riveting glimpses into the dangerous and grueling everyday world of nineteenth century African American and white Southwestern industrial workers. The author also pays attention to these workers' voting behavior and their complicated relationship to party and place in the recently "redeemed" South. And, finally and most impressively, she successfully opens for examination their ideology/culture of "free labor."

Case introduces the world of nineteenth-century American workers from the upheavals of the 1870s through the promise and disappointments of the 1880s to the straitened realities of the 1890s. The bulk of the work concerns the Southwestern railroad workers' uprisings of 1885 and 1886, and provides greater clarity of detail and analysis than any preceding work on this theme. More importantly, no previous work successfully places worker decisions, both individual and collective, within the context of nineteenth-century American free labor ideology.

It is difficult to imagine a more thorough use of the available sources. The author consulted relevant local newspapers from Kansas, Missouri, Arkansas, and Texas, as well as trade union organs, paper collections and the correspondence of main actors, and critical government documents. The work is also broadly informed by historians' writings on nineteenth-century worker culture.

It is a relief to find good readable prose in an academic monograph. While only a faint hope for most academic monographs, this book is so well-written as to be accessible to the general reading public.

Case begins with the daunting reality of late-nineteenth century railroad workers' daily regimen. From the best-paid locomotive engineers to the most heavily exploited member of a track maintenance crew, the daily work was difficult; costly to life and limb and, except for shopmen, often required extended periods away from home.

The author makes plain the racial hierarchy at work within worker culture, with the most skilled positions jealously guarded by the white aristocrats of labor. But, perhaps not so ironically, white and black workers found common ground in jealously guarding entry into railroading by Chinese workers and leased convicts, based both on wage concerns as well as ethnic bigotry.

Case then explores the rise of the Knights of Labor, attending the seemingly spectacular victory against Jay Gould in the 1885 Wabash strike. Thereafter, Knights' locals along Gould's lines grew rapidly to the delight of local unionists, but also brought dire predictions of too-rapid expansion by the order's always cautious Terrance Powderly. However, the explosion in growth could not be stopped due to the optimism following what appeared to be a resounding labor victory in 1885.

The victory was short-lived and could not be repeated in the 1886 strike for two reasons. First, the Gould railroads systematically broke the spirit and the letter of the 1885 contract. Gould and his leadership knew the contract could not be adequately enforced by the Knights (growing quickly but without deep roots and torn by internal weaknesses), and would never be enforced by state power or the courts. Indeed, the railroad managers knew that the courts and the coercive power of state government were at their disposal should they seek a confrontation.

The second reason 1886 failed, according to the author, is that the Knights exceeded the limits of "anti-monopoly," cross-class, community support they had enjoyed in 1885. Building upon the work of pioneers like Herbert Gutman, Case makes a signal contribution with her lucid examination of the tension between the ideology of individual workers' rights (broadly supported within local communities), and the collective rights of workers together. There had been widespread support among the community press, other skilled workers, farmers, and small merchants class for the right of workers to walk off the job and seek to defeat the monopolistic Gould in 1885. But, in 1886, when the fiery Southwestern strike leader, Martin Irons, and many Knights actively sought to shut down the railroads' operation (through moral persuasion, disabling of engines and threats of and actual violence), middle class support went away.

It is in interpreting this moment that the author materially expands our understanding of nineteenth-century America, as well as the world of the Southwestern worker in 1886 and after. Case brings her highly analytical narrative beyond the bitter defeat of 1886 to explore the tenuous "bi-racialism" of Southwestern Knights, delving into white workers' culture of white supremacy on the one hand, as well as the use of that culture by elites successfully seeking to maintain a fragmented and more easily controlled working class. The author also does a good job of looking at the same issue from the wary perspective of black workers caught in a devil's dilemma. Her nuanced grasp of nineteenth-century American racism and race relations is particularly rich; readers will benefit from the care she takes in exploring labor's painfully ambiguous struggle with America's original sin.

Kyle Wilkison
Collin College

Book Reviews

Calvin Littlejohn: Portrait of a Community in Black and White, by Bob Ray Sanders (TCU Press, P. O. Box 298300, Ft. Worth, TX 76129), 2009. Contents. Acknowledgements. Foreword. Introduction. List of Images. P. 200. $29.95. Hardcover.

The Jim Crow Era created many institutions, customs, and occupations in America in general, and the African American community in particular. One of these occupations was the African American photojournalist-documentarian. Calvin Littlejohn in Fort Worth served in that role, as did many others in all of the major cities in Texas with sizable African American communities. They captured life in the African American community not seen by the white community. They photographed school activities, church celebrations, business meetings, national leaders, community events, and sports and entertainment. Bob Ray Sanders, Senior Columnist and Associate Editor of the *Fort Worth Star Telegram*, with the help of Littlejohn family members, has organized select photographs taken by Calvin Littlejohn and featured them in a book that captures African American life at a significant time in Fort Worth.

Calvin Littlejohn came to Fort Worth in 1934 as a domestic servant in the home of a white family. Because of his self-training in photography, he eventually opened a studio and simultaneously became the official photographer for I.M. Terrell High School, the only African American high school in Fort Worth that could trace its origin back to the East Ninth Street Colored School founded in 1882. In the section of the book on schools, photo images date back to 1948. These images depict football games, band activities, pep rallies, proms, and beauty contests.

In the section of the book on businesses in the African American community, Littlejohn's images depict a vibrant business community, which operated not just hamburger and barbecue joints but a major bank (Fraternal Bank and Trust), hotel (Jim Hotel), taxicab companies, hospitals, and pharmacies. Prominent professionals from the medical and legal communities are portrayed. This volume includes a rare photo of Bill "Gooseneck" McDonald, one of the most prominent African American businessmen in Texas history.

Community life in the African American community was very similar to the white community—sororities, fraternities, lodges, literary clubs, nightclubs, and churches. Littlejohn took photographs of the first class of African Americans to graduate from the Police School in Fort Worth in 1951. In this section of the book, Sanders highlights Littlejohns's images of parades sponsored by the National Urban League, Boy Scout troops, and other community oriented activities.

As in most African American communities, the church played a prominent role. In Fort Worth, churches served as "not just places of worship, each was a refuge, a security zone, a solid rock in a land that sometime seemed alien for a people who faced constant discrimination," (p. 127). Littlejohn's images include church dedications, musicals, weddings, and important religious leaders.

Because Fort Worth has a sizeable African American community, nationally known entertainers performed on a regular basis. Littlejohn captured images of such luminaries as Ruth Brown, Duke Ellington, and Cab Calloway. Also featured are images of Nat "King" Cole, T-Bone Walker, Lionel Hampton, Oscar Peterson, Ella Fitzgerald, and others. From the world of sports are images of Jackie Robinson, Joe Louis, Mohammed Ali, and others.

Over the years, many national leaders visited Fort Worth. Among the images captured by Littlejohn were Paul Robeson, Thurgood Marshall, Ralph Bunche, Martin Luther King, Jr., and Jesse Jackson. Littlejohn also photographed white leaders when they addressed African American audiences in Fort Worth.

In summary, *Calvin Littlejohn: Portrait of a Community In Black and White* is an excellent book that helps preserve the history and culture of the African American community in Fort Worth. Although the book focuses on Fort Worth, it reflects the growth and development of typical African American communities throughout East Texas. Special thanks go to author Bob Ray Sanders and the Dolph Briscoe Center for American History at the University of Texas in Austin for having the foresight to undertake this project.

Theodore M. Lawe
A.C. McMillan
African American Museum
Emory, Texas

Book Reviews

The Polio Years In Texas: Battling a Terrifying Unknown, by Heather Green Wooten (Texas A&M University Press, 4354 TAMU, College Station, TX 77843-4354), 2009. List of tables, figures, and illustrations. Introduction. Appendices. Notes. Bibliography. P. 248. $19.95. Paperback.

For those of us who suffered from polio in that dark era, it was indeed "terrifying." If you survived the first week or so (and most did), it meant an indefinite period of recuperation, marked by exposure to the unfolding treatment of the day. To a kid, three months in a hospital could be forever, but the disease plagued some for an entire lifetime. And, in view of the recognition of a post-polio syndrome, thousands today face recurrence of complications.

Just remembering those days before the development of a polio vaccine is painful. That's why Heather Wooten's book is important. Most of the population today has no memory of polio and its heritage. Thanks to her work, which took about five years to complete, Texans may gain some idea of what polio meant. In tandem with David O'Shinsky's Pulitzer-Prize winning *Polio: An American Story* (2005), Wooten's study pinpoints the suffering that occurred in our state from the early part of the 20th century through the mid-1950s when a vaccine emerged.

Although medical researchers had some knowledge of polio's existence before the modern era, they had virtually no understanding of its cause or how it should be treated. Indeed, this modern plague shocked the nation when New York experienced an epidemic in 1916. Then known as infantile paralysis, polio showed up elsewhere in the following years, but it was not until the mid-1930s that epidemics became widespread.

With the coming of World War II and the resultant population shifts, polio continued its devastating tolls. Texas experienced several bad years in the later 1940s, especially in 1948 and 1949 (my sister and I became victims in August of 1948.) As Wooten notes, "Between 1942 and 1955, the disease struck hundreds of Texas communities, with the most devastating outbreak occurring in 1952. . . . Each year frightened parents prayed for a cure" (57). Indeed, every year from 1948 through 1956, more than a thousand Texans suffered polio attacks, with 1952 recording a total of 3,984 victims. (A national count revealed nearly

58,000 cases that year.) Harris County alone recorded 706 cases in 1952, including 439 in Houston (121). It was a good year for iron lungs and wheelchairs.

In addition to surveying the impact of polio on Texas, Wooten devotes considerable attention to treatment, fundraising, and the search for a vaccine. She rightfully focuses on Franklin D. Roosevelt, who was badly crippled by polio in 1921. He overcame his handicap and later became president. He ultimately became a "hero and role model for thousands of polio survivors and their families" (30).

Thanks to FDR, the treatment for polio received a boost beginning with his establishment in the mid-1920s of the Warm Springs, Georgia, Hospital for Rehabilitation. Subsequently, and with the aid of his business partner Basil O'Connor, he became prominent in the development of the National Foundation for Infantile Paralysis, which led to systematic fundraising (the March of Dimes) and assistance in treating polio. Every polio victim and all future generations benefited from such philanthropic activities that ultimately resulted in the discovery of a vaccine in the 1950s by Dr. Jonas Salk.

Wooten's work originally served as her doctoral dissertation at the University of Texas Medical Research Branch at the University of Texas at Galveston. Her study is based on a variety of sources, including numerous archival collections, oral history interviews, newspapers, and secondary works. She brilliantly portrays the human suffering and determination of those who endured a disease that no longer exists in our state or hemisphere. Except for isolated places in third world countries, polio has been defeated. In 2009, she won the Fehrenbach award from the Texas Historical Commission and the Ottis Lock award from the East Texas Historical Association, both for best books. It is a book that deserves reading.

Bobby H. Johnson
Nacogdoches, Texas

Farm Workers and the Churches: The Movement in California and Texas, by Alan J. Watt (Texas A&M University Press, 4354 TAMU, College Station, TX 77843), 2010. Contents. Acknowledgment. Introduction. Notes. Bibliography. Index. P.252. $24.00. Softcover.

Alan J. Watt's Farm Workers and the Churches is a comparative religious study chronicling the effectiveness of two farm worker strikes, one in California and one in Texas. In September 1965, Cesar Chavez and the United Farm Workers Union launched a strike and boycott against table grape growers in Delano, California, forcing the latter into contract negotiations and resulting in a union victory. Unlike the UFW California strike and boycott, the June 1966 Lower Rio Grande Valley wildcat melon strike was a dismal failure.

Locating his revisionist study in the context of New Western History and resource mobilization theory, Watt delineates how religious dimensions—traditional and liberal Protestantism, institutional Catholicism, and popular religion—intersected with economic, political, and demographic realities in two distinct regions and ultimately accounted for success in the California farm worker movement but failure in Texas.

Watt debunks religious scholarship that interprets Southwestern religious traditions as based solely on New England Puritanical orthodoxy and the single foundation for our Judeo-Christian faith. Specifically, Watt's religious treatise not only allows for the east-west and north-south migration of religious dogma but also accounts for multidirectional movements of that orthodoxy. For example, Watt shows how Northern Protestant sects, who espoused a socially conscious liberal theology, proselytized a Social Gospel seeking social and political institutional reforms.

Consequently, Northern Protestants sects, along with the pro-Union liberal supporters of the Roman Catholic Church, provided unwavering support for La Causa. In the California grape strike and boycott, Watt attributes its success not only to the role of liberal Protestantism and the institutional Roman Catholic Church but also to Chavez's ingenious ability to invoke nationalist-cultural symbols and Mexican devotional Catholicism, which is a subcategory of Latina/o popular religion. Chavez also possessed the uncanny ability to intertwine his own spirituality with a nascent awakening of a Mexican-American self-consciousness that helped mobilize a cadre of college students, "new breed clergy," laity, nuns, priests, union leaders, politicos, college professors, and social activists that propelled a farm worker victory.

In Texas, Southern Protestantism and Roman Catholic orthodoxy—which mirrored the region's provincialism and conservative race relations that portended the strike's failure—proselytized a Social Gospel that promoted personal salvation more than institutional reform. That religious conservatism, along with the recruitment of Mexican strikebreakers, weak union organizational structure, vacillating union leadership, failure to clarify the strike's objectives, entrenched racism, the Texas Rangers infamous reputation as an arm of the agribusiness, and anti-labor legislation crippled the farm workers' efforts in the melon strike. Although the farm worker movement failed, Watt contends, "it contributed to a series of events that led to a greater sense of self-determination [the Chicano/a Movement] among Mexican Americans in Texas" (161).

Watt traces the evolution of the roles of Protestant and Catholic Churches in the farm workers' struggle for social justice as they evolved from service to advocacy and finally to servanthood. In the initial decades of the twentieth century, the Catholic Church targeted religious instruction and the social welfare of farm workers through Catholic Charities and the Social Action Department. Meanwhile, the Protestant Church worked through the Migrant Ministry of the Council of Women on Home Missions. In the post-World II era, the Catholic Church and the Protestant Church shifted their focus from service to advocacy. The Catholic Church supported farm workers through its Social Action Department, the National Catholic Rural Life Conference, and the Bishops' Committee of the Spanish-Speaking and the Protestant Church through its National Council of Churches and the Migrant Ministry. Together they advocated for legislation to address the plight of farm workers and legally challenged the Bracero Program. Finally, while the institutional Catholic Church kept a lukewarm relationship with grower organizations, the Protestant Church—through the Migrant Ministry's community organizing and the unrelenting efforts of "new breed ministers"—adopted a servanthood form of ministry, placing them at the disposal of the farmworker.

Watt's monograph makes a compelling argument on religion's role in the farm worker movement and how the struggle impacted the Chicanas/os quest for civil rights. Another noteworthy feature of Watt's book is the inclusion of various personalities, whose names have escaped the historical record. This well-researched and superbly crafted monograph is a provocative and engaging study that merits the attention of religious, labor, Chicana/o, and borderlands scholars.

David Urbano
Victoria, Texas

Texas Through Women's Eyes: The Twentieth-Century Experience, by Judith N. McArthur and Harold L. Smith (University of Texas Press, P.O. Box 7819, Austin, TX), 2010. Contents. Acknowledgements. Notes. Index. P. 295. $24.95. Softcover.

Most early literature on Texas women centered on the nineteenth-century pioneer generation, who immigrated, settled, and adapted to frontier conditions. Only recently have scholars of both Texas history in general and women's history in particular refocused their historical lens on the modern, post-1900 era. Utilizing themes of reform, politics, suffrage, race, family, and feminism, historians Judith N. McArthur and Harold L. Smith at the University of Houston, Victoria, examine the "New Woman's century" which marked the emergence of a public female role in the twentieth century.

The objectives of *Texas Through Women's Eyes* are twofold: "to synthesize the existing scholarship and to map the historical terrain" (xiii). The authors, therefore, divide the book into four parts that conform to standard chronologies found in other texts. Part One covers the first two decades of the twentieth century, generally referred to as the Progressive Era. During that time, Texas women entered the workforce and professions in larger numbers, organized for multiple reforms, and claimed the right to vote. Part Two discusses the post-suffrage era from the 1920s to World War II. The achievement of the ballot, however, did not transform the entrenched political system; and Texas women continued to be excluded from jury service and equal employment protection. The depression decade, 1929-1939, affected all Texas women, regardless of race or ethnicity, while the New Deal programs only marginally helped women. Men generally got the jobs "while women were more likely to get direct relief and welfare." (88) Although sexual segregation in the workforce broke down during World

War II, the reconversion to peacetime forced many Texas women out of the workforce. Part Three, which covers the turbulent 1945-1965 period, contrasts the cultural emphasis on domesticity after the war with the advances by Texas women on many fronts—civil, legal, and employment. In the last section, covering the years 1965-2000, the authors document the emergence of a new feminist movement to combat continued job discrimination, wage inequality, and restrictive laws. However, Texas women did not always speak with one voice, and instead supported competing goals. Consequently, a backlash by conservative women's groups, such as the Texas Right to Life and the Committee to Restore Women's Rights, mobilized against the new morality of the sexual revolution. They lobbied against the Equal Rights Amendment, abortion rights, and sex education in public schools. The emergence of activist women on both the political right and left culminated in the splintering of the two factions at the 1977 Houston Women's Conference. So, century's end saw Texas women divided, and the tensions between the two factions remained "unresolved and seemingly irreconcilable" (138).

Texas Through Women's Eyes is a well-researched, thoughtful, and thorough analysis of women's experiences in the twentieth century. It combines in one volume a synthesis of women's lives, achievements, successes, failures, and divisions. While the authors include women from all racial, ethnic, and socio-economic backgrounds, the emphasis of the volume is primarily on urban, working to middle class, politically-active women. Considering that Texas was a rural state until 1940, farm women—who composed the majority of the female population for almost half of the century—are underrepresented. Nevertheless, the book should be essential reading for anyone interested in Texas and women's history during the modern era. The addition of vivid firsthand accounts to support the narrative further enhances the volume. Most importantly, this award-winning book fills a much-needed void in the literature and will be an important source for information about twentieth-century Texas women for a long time to come.

Mary L. Scheer
Lamar University

Don't Make Me Go to Town: Ranchwomen of the Texas Hill Country, by Rhonda Lashley Lopez (University of Texas Press, P.O. Box 7819, Austin, TX 78713-7819), 2011. Contents. Preface. Acknowledgements. Notes. P. 188. $24.66. Hardcover.

    Screen adaptations and fiction have long constructed a specific image of the typical Texas ranch, not to mention the stories told around a campfire on a cold night or those spun from a front porch swing on a hot summer's day. The presence of the strong human guardian is often a recurring theme in such forms and takes center stage to create a romantic and captivating hero for the listener or reader to enjoy. Rhonda Lashley Lopez provides the reader with factual stories of real women who took the reins of their ranching world and, in their own words, creates accounts that detail the ups and downs of earning a living from ranching.

    The book's subjects occupy a range of ages. Many of the women of an advanced age still do a long day's work with hard physical labor. Their knowledge is not considered old fashioned in the least and parallels quite nicely with the younger generation of ranchwomen. Some of the younger women are college educated. One young ranchwoman worked in Washington as a legislative intern, but she still intends to ranch for a living, despite the hardships. She expects to remain politically active because, in her mind, it is important that legislators and leaders receive input from those who actually practice agriculture daily and understand the challenges faced by such a lifestyle.

    The dreams and accounts of determination in this volume bear witness to the qualities necessary to be a successful ranchwoman. As one woman stated matter of factly, "You have to be hard-headed or persistent or tenacious, or you don't accomplish what you need to do. You give up" (83). Work on a ranch is never ending and requires an individual who can be both resourceful and strong. Each of these oral histories reveals a strength of character and spirit that engages the reader from the start. Lashley Lopez began this project in the late 1990s while working on a graduate degree in journalism/photojournalism, but after accumulating oral histories from these dedicated women, she continued her work and turned the project into the current book. She believed from the beginning that this was an important record of the changing way of ranch life—a lifestyle that had persisted generation after generation, change after change—and the documentation of such a transformation became increasingly important as the way of life slowly vanished. Readers will also understand the meaning of the title as they finish this fine work.

Leslie Daniel
Nacogdoches, Texas

History Ahead: Stories beyond the Texas Roadside Markers, by Dan K. Utley and Cynthia J. Beeman (Texas A&M University Press, 4354 TAMU, College Station, TX 77843), 2010. Contents. Foreword. Acknowledgements. Introduction. Notes. Index. P. 317. $23.00. Softcover.

The long work of creating historical markers dotting the Lone Star State began in 1932 when a constitutional amendment created the Texas Centennial Commission. In 1953 work continued under the auspice of the Texas State Historical Survey Committee, which changed its name to the Texas Historical Commission (THC) in 1973. In fact, Texas boasts the most state markers of any in the U.S. with more than one to two hundred markers positioned each year. Still, little is written about this bigger-in-Texas movement to commemorate, and educate about, the past. Besides the phenomenal collection in *Lone Star Pasts: Memory and History in Texas* (edited by Gregg Cantrell and Elizabeth H. Turner, 2007) and James E. Crisp's excellent work on the Alamo and Davy Crockett (*How Did Davy Die? And Why Do We Care So Much*, with Dan Kilgore, 2010; and *Sleuthing the Alamo: Davy Crockett's Last Stand and Other Mysteries of the Texas Revolution*, 2005), surprisingly little is written on the process of history in the public in Texas, especially compared to other large states like California and New York. Now, thankfully, Dan K. Utley (former chief historian of THC) and Cynthia J. Beeman (former director of THC) provide a corrective turn. With a much deserved tip-of-the-hat to their writing, Utley and Beeman "explore the diverse history of Texas as told through its state markers" (x-xi).

Identifying historical markers as "iconic elements of the modern cultural landscape," Utley and Beeman unpack the dynamic history behind more than nineteen state markers, as well as provide numerous "side bars" to complement each chapter that "are the defining components of cultures and societies" (1). From the woods of Elmer Kelb outside Houston to the mysterious lights of Marfa in the high desert of West Texas, the stories behind the markers speak to both the diversity and the plethora of history in Texas.

History Ahead is divided into three parts. Part One ("A Texas Sense of Place") marks, as it were, the crafting of a sense of place rooted in history. Following the stories of forest conservation, real-estate speculation, King Cotton, faith healing, oil, religion, and even a music director, "A Texas Sense of Place" is concerned "with both the places where history was made, and the individuals who made it" (54). Part Two ("Passing Through Texas") looks to the storied many who, while not exactly Texan (to which Utley and Beeman are wise not to hold such against them), found their way to Texas and, yet again, reveal the intimate connections of history making to Texas' past. American icons Charles Lindbergh and Will Rogers stand next to conservationists in Tyler, failed entrepreneurs in Marfa, utopists along the Ozark Trails, and internees and POWs at Crystal City during World War II. They all, without doubt, highlight the "basics of a national story that began in Texas" (189)—or if not beginning in Texas then visited nonetheless—and tell a story that moves beyond state boundaries. Part Three ("Texans on the National Stage") exposes the effect Texans have had not just in their home state but also around the nation and world. A female progressive reformer, bluesman, literary scholar, aviator, rock n' roller, and theater magnet give just a small glimpse into the larger world Texans both traversed and helped shape.

The stories behind the markers are more than just vignettes into the remarkable, sometimes untold, stories of the past—or as another reviewer called them "the state's oddballs" (back cover of *History Ahead*). Rather, beyond the rich histories told in this work, two other aspects render it truly valuable: diversity and public history in Texas. Utley and Beeman provide a history that unquestionably captures the diverse landscape of Texas. The stories of Charles Lindbergh and Will Rogers flow seamlessly with the stories of Bessie Coleman, a female African-American aviator, and Carl T. Morene, a self-educated working-class white man from Schulenburg. Stories from Dallas and Houston also accompany stories of towns that no longer exist or are tucked away in the rural pine curtain of East Texas. These are all the faces and landscapes of a diverse and lively Texas.

Moreover, *History Ahead* will prove very useful to those interested in cultural resources management, historic preservation, memory, and public history in Texas. Utley and Beeman present insights into what history making in the public looks like in practice and, again, in Texas. Often accompanying the history of the people, places, and events behind a state marker is the history to create the state marker itself – the people involved; their motivations; and, more importantly, the meanings they ascribe to their markers. Put differently, *History Ahead* reveals how Texans have looked to take ownership of their own past and, in the process, makes known to readers just what Texans decide is important about both themselves and their community.

As with *Lone Star Pasts* and Crisp's work, Utley and Beeman provide a snapshot into the ways Texans have gone about quite literally marking a sense of their own identity. This book is nothing shy of a detailed chronicling of the construction of historical identity in and throughout Texas. Moreover, *History Ahead* (not surprisingly with two authors from THC) provides insight into the issues of marking preservation and commemoration. They chronicle the not always smooth history of historic preservation efforts, the hard work by individuals to create the places and markers Texans now enjoy, and the life of a place after a noted person or event has long left or receded from popular memory. Particularly notable is the importance of local activity and initiative to history making in Texas—as elsewhere to be sure. *History Ahead* repeatedly spotlights individuals and communities that took history into their own hands. Equally intriguing are the small glimpses into the inner workings of THC as it struggled to define standards and then balance these standards with local populist needs to find meaning and ascribe local significance. *History Ahead* then is more than a story of oddballs—no matter how fascinating they truly are; it is the story of how history is made and what the past can mean for people in the present and future.

Paul J. P. Sandul
Stephen F. Austin State University

State of Minds: Texas Culture and Its Discontents, by Don Graham

(University of Texas Press, P.O. Box 7819, Austin, TX 78713), 2011. Bibliography. Credits. P. 183. $29.95. Hardback.

As its title indicates, University of Texas literary professor Don Graham's latest book attempts to justify John Steinbeck's famous line, "Texas is a state of mind." Through his well-crafted and witty critiques of Texas authors and filmmakers, Graham demonstrates how popular culture shaped the image of the Lone Star State in the minds of both outsiders and native Texans.

Graham's book is a compilation of nineteen articles previously published in *Texas Monthly*, as well as various other journals and edited books published between 1999 and 2009. Graham claims to have made numerous updates and revisions to each of the included articles, but readers familiar with the author's writings may find themselves wishing for new and updated material. That being said, anyone with little or no pervious contact with Graham's work will quickly be taken in by his extremely entertaining writing style.

Lovers of Texas movies will find Graham's three essays on the motion picture industry particularly interesting. In his essay "Wayne's World," Graham suggests, "Davy Crockett became a Texan by dying at the Alamo, and John Wayne became a Texan by making *The Alamo*" (124). In the second essay that deals with Texas movies, Graham provides readers with an edited transcript of his interviews with several key players behind the production of the 1971 classic Texas film *The Last Picture Show*. The author ends his look at Texas films with a highly entertaining discussion on the evolution of the Hollywood cowboy in the movie *Brokeback Mountain*.

The majority of Graham's essays focus on Texas literature. Over the course of the book, Graham introduces little known Texas authors and reacquaints readers with some of the state's most influential writers. Having taught the famed course "Life and Literature of the Southwest" at the University of Texas for over three decades, Graham is uniquely qualified to comment on the subject of Texas writing. One of the many interesting opinions on Texas literature that Graham presents in his essays is that cotton—not cattle or oil—provided the driving influence behind some of the Lone Stat State's greatest works of fiction. Graham is particularly fond of the writing of Larry McMurtry and calls his first novel, *Horseman, Pass By*, the Texas version of *Catcher in the Rye*. On the other hand, Graham is not quite as kind to Cormac McCarthy and suggests McCarthy's Hollywood success may have gone to his head.

Scholars seeking a better understanding of the history of Texas in popular culture and literature cannot help but run into the writings of Don Graham. More than any other professional, Graham has shaped this underdeveloped field, and *State of Minds* fits nicely into his extensive list of published works. However, the book offers little in terms of new information. The essays included have previously been published elsewhere, and most can be easily accessed through a simple Internet search. Graham missed an opportunity to expand on his work, as well as a chance to advance the literature of Texas cultural history. In addition, the book fails to include any type of conclusion. Without a concluding chapter, readers finish the book wondering exactly how Graham's assortment of essays ties into his introductory argument. Despite its numerous shortcomings, readers with an interest in Texas cultural history who are not already familiar with Graham's work owe it to themselves to take a look at this informative and entertaining book.

Preston Blevins
Nacogdoches, Texas

Americo Paredes: In His Own Words, An Authorized Biography, by Manuel F. Medrano (University of North Texas Press, 1155 Union Circle #311336, Denton, TX 76203), 2010. Notes. Bibliography. Index. P. 224. $22.95. Hardcover.

In 1999, students and academics mourned the death of renowned scholar and University of Texas at Austin professor Americo Paredes. Born in Brownsville, Texas, Paredes spent his career celebrating the diversity and richness of border culture. His works, which include *With His Pistol in His Hand: A Border Ballad and its Hero* (1958), *A Texas Mexican Cancionero: Folksongs of the Lower Border* (1976), and *George Washington Gomez: A Mexicotexan Novel* (1990), contributed to the development of Mexican American/Chicano scholarship and studies. The influence of Paredes' writings has been the subject of several studies. For instance, Jose R. Lopez Morin's *The Legacy of Americo Paredes* (2006) explores the impact of Paredes' writings on the evolution of Mexican American cultural scholarship.

While the work of Lopez Morin and others examines the significance of Paredes' scholarship, Manuel F. Medrano, professor of history at the University of Texas at Brownsville, provides readers with a look at the life of a humble man who inspired many. *Americo Paredes: In His Own Words, an Authorized Biography* traces the life of Paredes from his childhood in South Texas to his activities after retirement. Utilizing interviews with Paredes, his family, and friends, Medrano shows the triumphs, as well as the difficulties, Paredes experienced.

As a young boy, Paredes spent hours listening to his mother as she regaled him with stories (such as the tale of Mexican folk hero Gregorio Cortez) that inspired in him a love for storytelling. During summers Paredes visited his uncle's ranch near Matamoros, Tamaulipas, where he heard border tales and folk ballads, including those associated with Catarino Garza. Paredes' father, Justo Paredes Cisneros, joined Garza's 1891 rebellion against Mexican President Porfirio Diaz. Paredes' appreciation for border culture grew out of these childhood experiences.

Tracing his life through the depression and war years, during which Paredes enlisted and edited the *Pacific Stars and Stripes*, Medrano shows Paredes' dedication to writing and education. After the war Paredes earned a doctorate in English and folklore. His dissertation focused on the 1901 Gregorio Cortez incident, which found Cortez, a Mexican peasant, accused of horse theft and murder. Using Spanish-language border ballads, Paredes placed the Cortez affair in the context of Anglo-Mexican relations and border conflict. Paredes was rebuked for his criticism of renowned folklorist Walter Prescott Webb and the Texas Rangers. Paredes' study brought to light the abuse Mexicans suffered at the hand of the Rangers, which challenged Webb's portrayal of the Rangers as a just frontier agency and the Mexican people as inherently cruel and treacherous.

Despite these objections the University of Texas Press published Paredes' dissertation, *With His Pistol in His Hand: A Border Ballad and Its Hero*. During an interview with Medrano, Paredes recalled that despite a UT Press tradition of hosting a book signing event for newly-released books, the publication of *With His Pistol in His Hand* received no such fanfare. Publication of *With His Pistol in His Hand* coincided with the rise of the Chicano Movement and served as a catalyst for the study of Mexican American/Chicano culture and folklore.

Among Paredes' many achievements was the creation of The

Center for Mexican American Studies (CMAS) at UT in 1970, which recognized the importance of the Mexican-American experience. Paredes continued to produce significant works after his retirement and received many honors, including the Order of the Aztec Eagle from the Mexican government in 1990 and a life-time achievement award from the Texas legislature in 1998.

Medrano celebrates Paredes' professional accomplishments by placing them within a general narrative of Paredes' personal life. An outstanding feature in Americo Paredes is the unedited transcription of the author's interview with Paredes in which Paredes details his childhood, his struggle to obtain a higher education, and the conflict over the creation of the CMAS. Despite the limited focus on Paredes' relationship with family and friends outside of academia, *Americo Paredes* is an excellent work that complements existing scholarship on the legendary scholar.

Ana Luisa Martinez-Catsam
The University of Texas of the Permian Basin

Constructing the Image of the Mexican Revolution: Cinema and the Archive, by Zuzana M. Pick (University of Texas Press, P.O. Box 7819, Austin, TX 78713), 2010. Contents. Acknowledgements. Notes. Bibliography. Index. P. 253. $55.00. Hardcover.

Mexican modern identity, argues Zuzana M. Pick, is not part of an "absolute break" from the past but rather involves "a cultural and discursive rearrangement of the already existing visual signifiers of nation, identity, and modernity" (5). This includes both the ideas of "mexicanidad" at home, as well as stereotypes of Mexico found abroad – particularly in the United States. This discourse, she argues, uses archival images and films that serve to create the image of Mexico through the twentieth and into the twenty-first centuries on topics like violence, gender, and urban landscapes. This is important, argues the author, because it sets Mexican identity formation squarely outside of European models of modernity as has been argued by past works on the subject. Mexico and Mexicans have decided what it means to project their sense of identity and modernity, not external forces.

Pick examines key images and films through seven chapters and argues that archival images, when compared to cinematic theater and promotional films, show how Mexico has been imagined and re-imagined through visual media. Of particular importance are foundational films from the Mexican Revolution or those created as a result of the conflict: chapter one covers landmark documentaries, such as *Memorias de un Mexicano* (Carmen Toscano de Moreno Sánchez, 1950); chapter two looks at films that address the work *The Life of General Villa* (now-lost); chapter three compares views of Villa from the U.S. and Mexico in *Viva Villa!* (Jack Conway, U.S., 1933) and *¡Vámonos con Pancho Villa!* (Fernando de Fuentes, 1935); chapter four looks at Sergei Eisenstein's classic 1930s film *Que Viva México!* as edited by Grigori Alexandrov (1979); chapter five examines golden-age melodrama with *las abandonadas* (Emilio "El Indio" Fernández, 1944); chapter six analyzes films dealing with aesthetics of spectacle, such as the *The Wild Bunch* (Sam Peckinpah, U.S., 1969); and in chapter seven she dives into films about foreigners transformed by Mexico with *Reed: Insurgent Mexico* (Paul Leduc, Mexico, 1971) about American communist and journalist John Reed and Tina in Mexico (Brenda Longfellow, 2001) about actress and photographer Tina Modotti.

One of the best ideas discussed by Pick is the paradox of the creation of film as a "freezing" of the Mexican Revolution into bits of controllable celluloid, a project conducive to the United States and the ruling party (PRI), as well as cues of memory to those millions of Mexicans who participated. Because so many Mexicans experienced the Revolution as either a producer or a recipient of its violence, the uprising inevitably becomes a site of uncontrolled meaning. For example, the presence of female soldaderas and indigenous rebels in images might either remind the viewer that the Revolution promised liberation or that it had not yet delivered on those same promises.

While the author is successful in her argument, Pick writes for an audience that is familiar with Mexico, the Revolution, and film theory; and this is not a book lightly picked up for general audiences with a casual interest in film or the Mexican Revolution. Indeed, those interested in history and use of Mexican film and less interested in the jargon of film theory would be better served by reading Seth Fein, professor of American Studies at Yale, who has published on film in the post-revolutionary period, or Thomas Benjamin and Ilene V. O'Malley, both imminently respectable and authors on the production of Mexican identity during the Revolution. While Pick's work is of value for film studies and the idea of the creation of the image of Mexico, the work is less unique – though not uninformative – for historians of the Mexican Revolution, who are familiar with the cultural and political "repurposing" of cultural tropes that serve as sites of contested meaning.

Jason Dormady
Stephen F. Austin State University

Until They Are Home, Bringing Back the MIAs from Vietnam, a Personal Memoir, by Thomas T. Smith (Texas A&M University Press, 4354 TAMU, College Station, TX 77843), 2011. Contents. Introduction. Afterword. Index. P. 136. $29.95 Hardcover.

While the decision to take military action in Southeast Asia remains a hotly debated topic, the endeavor to locate and return the 2,585 missing United States military personnel reaffirmed an American commitment that exemplifies our humanity. Armed with a confection of pungent memories, Thomas T. Smith, a Vietnam veteran and Texan, returned to that country as the officer charged with command and control of the 1992-formed Joint Task Force-Full Accounting military organization. He distills the identification processes of the missing, and he sprinkles his serious-subject memoir with quotidian tales of cultural misunderstandings among his residence maids and staff, as well as relay the nuances of political protocols required for an overall successful mission. Although on duty most of the time, Thomas also donned a tourist hat and describes for the reader a communist country that remains culturally divided between approximately fifty-four tribal entities in the old French Colonial North and the Los Angeles-style, traffic-laden Saigon occupied by a separate ethnic group that flaunts its imagined racial superiority.

Thomas conveys a sense of duty, honor, and country without the over sentimentality that generally accompanies personal recollections. During his 2003-2004 assignment, Thomas artfully wove into his story elements of existentialism as defined by Albert Camus, Shakespearean references to fallen warriors, and Homeric examples and comparisons to the trials and tribulations of the journeys of Odysseus. Flavoring his classical illustrations with down-home Texas truisms, Thomas emphasizes the importance of handshakes and the avoidance of rattlesnakes! He prized candor when explaining the exact reasons for the "restricted" areas that prevented the search for some of those missing heroes. Vietnam suffered insurrections over political strife between traditional religious practices and the introduction of Christianity in the highlands.

Not only did the recovery process depend on tedious excavation methods and cutting-edge forensic anthropological techniques, serendipitous discoveries by locals provided the tips that determined potential recovery sites. Rife with rumors that the United States would pay a king's ransom or allow the holder of the secrets a chance for life in America, Thomas faced a daunting task. He understood the stakes of his mission; therefore, he gingerly negotiated the release of the remains held by local tribal families. He recognized early on that well-chosen words could illicit emotional outbursts and copious tears by many Vietnamese women, indicating that mothers and grandmothers held much sway with their family members as they convinced sons to give up their precious finds without those rumored rewards of money or trips to America. Transported to the laboratory in Hawaii, the remains were identified and repatriated for burial. Although peripheral to his main theme, he intimated his disgust for the remnants and residue of the infamous Khmer Rouge Prison S-21 that he found even more repulsive than his visit to Bergen-Belsen concentration camp in Germany. Readers will also enjoy his lighter tales of scary flights, rutted roads, a cake cut with a machete, and an attack of the leeches.

Fate often provides an avenue for humans to face those memories that seem best left behind—a time to jettison the flotsam that gnaws at the soul during the darkest nights. Thomas' "soft" journey allows those who served a vicarious insight into the twenty-first century countries of Vietnam, Laos, and Cambodia and how Americans and these Southeast Asians arrived at an uneasy reconciliation that benefited each country in dramatically different ways. The United States needed the remains of its citizen soldiers for closure; and these countries, although communist in organization, desired a venue into the world marketplace—what the State Department deemed a win-win. The Thomas book is also a win-win for all those who choose to share his touching and educational journey into an area of the world perceived by most Americans as a mysterious backwater with the issuance of the

1964 Gulf of Tonkin Resolution that gave President Lyndon Johnson his authority to put "boots on the ground" in Vietnam. Thomas "absorbed" a Vietnamese cultural belief that embracing the good while accepting the bad completes the circle of life. He and his various dedicated teams repatriated fourteen Americans—each name, each state origin, and each burial detailed. From all across America, though some were Texans and two were graduates of Texas A& M University, all finally home. This was Thomas' finest hour.

Cynthia Devlin
Stephen F. Austin State University

NEW BOOKS FROM TEXAS A&M

RUDDER
From Leader to Legend
THOMAS A. HATFIELD
In this first comprehensive biography of James Earl Rudder, Hatfield paints a full portrait of the man who exemplified leadership, vision, and courage, during the Normandy invasion, in the Texas Land Office, and as president of Texas A&M University.
528 pp. 68 b&w photos. 8 maps. Bib. Index. $30.00 cloth; $150.00 limited edition

TEJANOS IN GRAY
Civil War Letters of Captains Joseph Rafael de la Garza and Manuel Yturri
Edited and with an Introduction by JERRY THOMPSON
Translations by JOSÉ ROBERTO JUÁREZ
Gathered for the first time in this book, these letters reveal the intricate and intertwined relationships that characterized the lives of Texan citizens of Mexican descent in the years leading up to and including the Civil War.
160 pp. 12 b&w photos. Bib. Index. $29.95 cloth

New in paperback
JUAN DAVIS BLACKBURN
A Reappraisal of the Mexican Commander of Anahuac
MARGARET SWETT HENSON
$16.95s paper

BEYOND TEXAS THROUGH TIME
Breaking Away from Past Interpretations
Edited by WALTER L. BUENGER and ARNOLDO DE LEÓN
This new work—an extension of the seminal historiography work *Texas Through Time*—considers the topical and thematic understandings of Texas historiography embraced by a new generation of Texas historians as they reflect analytically on the work of the past two decades. 288 pp. 3 tables. Index. $45.00x cloth; $24.95s paper

Available again
TEXAS THROUGH TIME
Evolving Interpretations
WALTER L. BUENGER and ROBERT A. CALVERT
408 pp. Bib. Index. $28.50x paper

TEXAS A&M UNIVERSITY PRESS
800.826.8911 Fax: 888.617.2421 **www.tamupress.com**

Fall 2011
Stephen F. Austin

SHERBURNE

"Ranging through time from the Civil War to the present, this intricate and exquisitely written collection further confirms that R. T. Smith is one of America's best writers. Sherburne is a magnificent acheivement."
—Ron Rash

STORIES

R.T. SMITH

R. T. Smith is Writer-in-residence at Washington and Lee University. He has twice received the Library of Virginia Poetry Book of the Year Award and is the recipient of fellowships from the NEA, the Virginia Commission for the Arts and the Alabama State Arts Council. His work has appeared in Best American Poetry, Best American Short Stories, three editions of The Pushcart Prize

Fall 2011
State University Press

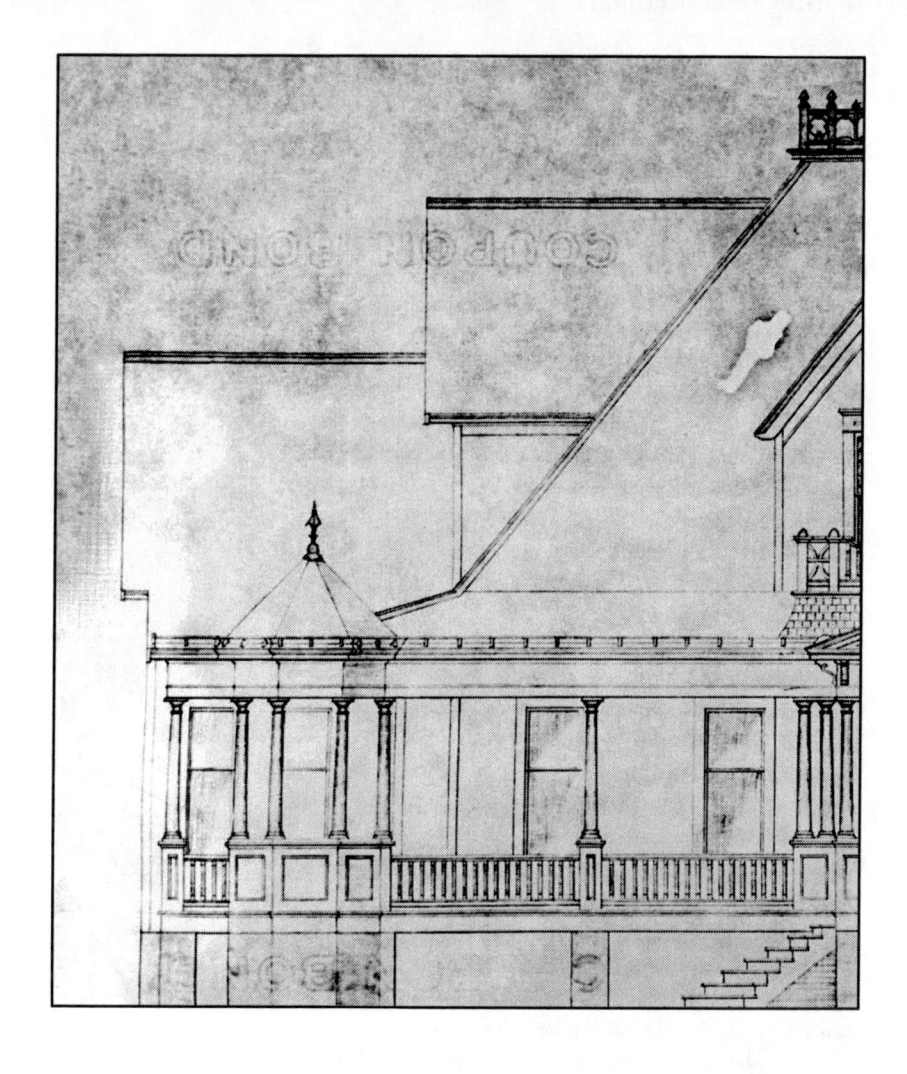

Diedrich Rulfs: Designing Modern Nacogdoches

AVAILABLE NOVEMBER 2011

Institutional Members

A.C. McMillan African American Museum, Emory
American Legion Post 3140, Longview
Angelina College, Lufkin
Bancorp South, Nacogdoches
Camp Ford Historical Association, Tyler
Cherokee County Historical Commission, Jacksonville
Commercial Bank of Texas, N.A., Nacogdoches
East Texas Baptist University, Marshall
East Texas Oil Museum, Kilgore
First Bank & Trust East Texas, Diboll-Lufkin-Nacogdoches
Harper Cooperative, Paris
Harris County Flood Control District, Houston
Harrison County Historical Commission, Marshall
Jacksonville College, Jacksonville
Kilgore College, Kilgore
Lamar University, Beaumont
LeTourneau University, Longview
Linda Frazier, Arlington
The Long Trusts, Kilgore
Midwestern State University, Wichita Falls
Northeast Texas Community College, Mount Pleasant
Peggy & Tome Wright, Nacogdoches
Panola College, Carthage
Red River Radio Network, Shreveport, Louisiana
Regions Bank, Nacogdoches
Sam Houston Regional Library & Research Center, Liberty
Sam Houston State University, Huntsville
San Jacinto College, North, Houston
San Jacinto Museum of History, La Porte
Southwest Dairy Museum, Sulphur Springs
Smith County Historical Society, Tyler
Temple-Inland Forest Products Corporation, Diboll
Texas Forestry Association, Lufkin
Texas Historical Commission, Austin
Thomas McCall, Bullard
Tyler Junior College, Tyler
Tyler Morning Telegraph, Tyler
University of Texas-San Antonio Department of History, San Antonio
Vinson & Elkins, L.L.P., Houston

And sponsored by Stephen F. Austin State University